Delivering Insurance Services

Delivering Insurance Services

Edited by

Mary Ann Cook, CPCU, MBA, AU, AAI

4th Edition • 1st Printing

The Institutes
720 Providence Road, Suite 100
Malvern, Pennsylvania 19355-3433

4th Edition • 1st Printing • December 2011

Library of Congress Control Number: 2011960431

ISBN 978-0-89463-492-5

Foreword

The Institutes are the trusted leader in delivering proven knowledge solutions that drive powerful business results for the risk management and property-casualty insurance industry. For more than 100 years, The Institutes have been meeting the industry's changing professional development needs with customer-driven products and services.

In conjunction with industry experts and members of the academic community, our Knowledge Resources Department develops our course and program content, including Institutes study materials. Practical and technical knowledge gained from Institutes courses enhances qualifications, improves performance, and contributes to professional growth—all of which drive results.

The Institutes' proven knowledge helps individuals and organizations achieve powerful results with a variety of flexible, customer-focused options:

Recognized Credentials—The Institutes offer an unmatched range of widely recognized and industry-respected specialty credentials. The Institutes' Chartered Property Casualty Underwriter (CPCU) professional designation is designed to provide a broad understanding of the property-casualty insurance industry. Depending on professional needs, CPCU students may select either a commercial insurance focus or a personal risk management and insurance focus and may choose from a variety of electives.

In addition, The Institutes offer certificate or designation programs in a variety of disciplines, including these:

- Claims
- Commercial underwriting
- Fidelity and surety bonding
- General insurance
- Insurance accounting and finance
- Insurance information technology
- Insurance production and agency management
- Insurance regulation and compliance
- Management
- Marine insurance
- Personal insurance
- Premium auditing
- Quality insurance services
- Reinsurance
- Risk management
- Surplus lines

Ethics—Ethical behavior is crucial to preserving not only the trust on which insurance transactions are based, but also the public's trust in our industry as a whole. All Institutes designations now have an ethics requirement, which is delivered online and free of charge. The ethics requirement content is designed specifically for insurance practitioners and uses insurance-based case studies to outline an ethical framework. More information is available in the Programs section of our Web site, www.TheInstitutes.org.

Flexible Online Learning—The Institutes have an unmatched variety of technical insurance content covering topics from accounting to under-writing, which we now deliver through hundreds of online courses. These cost-effective self-study courses are a convenient way to fill gaps in technical knowledge in a matter of hours without ever leaving the office.

Continuing Education—A majority of The Institutes' courses are filed for CE credit in most states. We also deliver quality, affordable, online CE courses quickly and conveniently through our newest business unit, CEU.com. Visit www.CEU.com to learn more.

College Credits—Most Institutes courses carry college credit recommendations from the American Council on Education. A variety of courses also qualify for credits toward certain associate, bachelor's, and master's degrees at several prestigious colleges and universities. More information is available in the Student Services section of our Web site, www.TheInstitutes.org.

Custom Applications—The Institutes collaborate with corporate customers to utilize our trusted course content and flexible delivery options in developing customized solutions that help them achieve their unique organizational goals.

Insightful Analysis—Our Insurance Research Council (IRC) division conducts public policy research on important contemporary issues in property-casualty insurance and risk management. Visit www.ircweb.org to learn more or purchase its most recent studies.

The Institutes look forward to serving the risk management and property-casualty insurance industry for another 100 years. We welcome comments from our students and course leaders; your feedback helps us continue to improve the quality of our study materials.

Peter L. Miller, CPCU
President and CEO
The Institutes

Preface

Delivering Insurance Services is the assigned textbook in The Institutes' Associate in Insurance Services (AIS) designation program. The program examines issues of continuous improvement and total quality from a unique insurance perspective. Entire departments of some insurers, as well as many insurance agencies, have transformed their businesses by embracing the models described here.

In this text, you will find that the total quality movement is more than a philosophy. Experts and practitioners alike have documented processes and metrics to help organizations advance in their commitment to continuous improvement.

The Institutes are deeply indebted to Dr. Warren Hope for his vision in designing this course. We must also thank the students and course leaders who convinced us of the need for this course and then helped us determine ways to improve it.

For more information about The Institutes' programs, please call our Customer Service Department at (800) 644-2101, e-mail us at customerservice@TheInstitutes.org, or visit our Web site at www.TheInstitutes.org.

Mary Ann Cook

Contributors

The Institutes acknowledge with deep appreciation the contributions made to the content of this text by the following persons:

Christopher J. Amrhein

Richard Berthelsen, Esq., MBA, CPCU

Pamela Brooks, MBA, CPCU, AIM

Howard E. Candage, CPCU, CIC, AIS

Mary Ann Cook, CPCU, MBA, AU, AAI

Mary E. Del Cueto, SPHR

Jay T. Deragon

Martin J. Frappolli, CPCU, FIDM, AIS

Frank J. Herberg, CPCU, AIS, AAM

James R. Jones, CPCU, AIC, ARM, AIS

Carla Kean Kutz, CPCU, API

C. (Neil) Mahoney, CPCU, AU, AIS

James Markham, Ph.D., J.D., CPCU

Ann Myhr, CPCU, ARM, ASLI, AU

John G. Pryor, CPCU, ARM, AIS

Jo Conway Roberts, CPIW

Peter Schriffrin

William N. Weld, CPCU, CLU, AIS

Lowell Young, CPCU, CLU, APA, AIAF

Richard Zanoni

Contents

1

The Nature of the Insurance Business

Educational Objectives

After learning the content of this assignment, you should be able to:

▸ Explain why insurance organizations are experimenting with quality initiatives.

▸ Explain how the characteristics of the insurance product influence customer satisfaction.

▸ Identify how the benefits of insurance relate to the personal experiences of consumers.

▸ Explain why insurance is classed as a service.

The Nature of the Insurance Business

1

QUALITY INITIATIVES IN ORGANIZATIONS

Insurance organizations are continually searching for ways to respond to an increasingly competitive business environment. Quality initiatives, including those related to knowledge of the language, tools, and ideas of continuous improvement; and development of interpersonal skills, can increase an organization's competitiveness.

Maintaining one's technical knowledge is virtually a requirement in today's business world. Equally as important, if not more so, are knowledge and information related to quality and continuous improvement. Organizations experiment with and implement quality initiatives as a means of improving service and responding to a changing environment.

In recent years, many insurance organizations have tried to change the way they do business. In some cases, this change has been initiated by an internal desire to improve the organization. In other cases, external forces—competitive, financial, or technological forces, usually—have made change a necessity. Either way, these insurance organizations are part of a broader movement in American business, a recognition of the need for "continuous improvement." Some observers call this movement the "**Quality Revolution**." The "revolution" began when the teachings of quality experts W. Edwards Deming and Joseph Juran gained adherents who achieved noteworthy results. See the exhibit "A Note From the History of Quality."

Quality initiatives frequently focus on **continuous improvement**, an organizational condition achieved by the use of these three elements: customer orientation, process improvement, and employee involvement.

The nature of the insurance industry presents certain challenges to the quality initiative effort. For example, insurance transactions can be examined from both an employee performance perspective and a continuous improvement perspective. See the exhibit "A Claim Against Insure-All."

These two differing analytical perspectives (employee performance and continuous improvement) could be applied to all transactions and are not peculiar to the insurance business. However, certain elements of the insurance transaction do present unique obstacles to delivering quality service, including the uniqueness of the product as well as the types of benefits it provides. See the exhibit "Reputation of the Insurance Business."

Quality Revolution

A broad term used to describe the shift in outlook among managers and executives of all kinds of organizations that arose with the growing realization that quality can be equated with customer satisfaction. This movement recognizes the need for continuous improvement of services.

Continuous improvement

The organizational condition achieved through (1) customer orientation, (2) process improvement, and (3) employee involvement.

A Note From the History of Quality

Over time, many thinkers have contributed to the history and development of continuous process improvement. One of these individuals is Joseph Juran.

Juran was born in what is now Romania and arrived in the United States at the age of nine, with no knowledge of English. He settled in Minnesota and learned not only English but also other subjects rapidly, later insisting that taking advantage of educational opportunities throughout life was the basis for his success. He earned a degree in electrical engineering from the University of Minnesota and a law degree.

Employed by Western Electric, the manufacturing arm of the Bell System, he became a member of the inspection department, a forerunner of the quality control function now present in many organizations. He rapidly gained a reputation for finding flaws in manufacturing processes and recommending ways to eliminate them. The pleasure he took in these investigations convinced him it would be possible to develop processes that would "get rid of the errors in the first place," rather than finding them through inspections and then fixing them.

Eventually Juran developed his ideas and conveyed them through what is known as the Juran Trilogy:

1. Quality planning: A process that (a) identifies the customers, their requirements, the product and service features the customers expect, and the processes that will deliver those products and services with the correct attributes and (b) facilitates the transfer of this knowledge to the producing arm of the organization.

2. Quality control: A process in which the product is actually examined and problems detected are then corrected.

3. Quality improvement: A process in which the sustaining mechanisms are put in place so that quality can be achieved on a continuous basis. This includes allocating resources, assigning people to pursue quality projects, training, and generally establishing a structure to pursue quality and to maintain the gains secured.

Joseph Juran, along with W. Edwards Deming, is generally credited with bringing the Quality Revolution to America.

[DA04413]

A Claim Against Insure-All

Case Scenario

Carl Atkins, a claim representative with Insure-All, a regional insurance company that primarily writes auto insurance, had an appointment at 10:00 a.m. on Tuesday with a third-party claimant and the claimant's attorney. Carl's intention to prepare for the meeting late Monday afternoon was not fulfilled because of numerous phone calls and an unexpected meeting with his supervisor on another case. He took the claim file home Monday night, hoping to review it there but was unable to find the time to do so. He arrived at the office early on Tuesday so that he would have time to prepare for the meeting.

With the claim file placed on his desk, Carl settled down to what he hoped would be a quiet half-hour of concentration. Negotiations with the claimant and attorney had been going well, and Carl had hoped that today they would accept the payment he would offer at the meeting and settle the claim. What Carl needed to do was gather some information on amounts paid to settle similar recent claims. He turned the computer on to search for the information.

Caroline Schroeder, Carl's supervisor, popped her head into Carl's cubicle and said, "We need to meet right away. The Wagner case is becoming a crisis."

"I've got a meeting at 10:00, Caroline," Carl said, "and I need to...."

"This will just take a few minutes, but it must be now."

Carl followed Caroline down the hall. When he returned to his desk, he thought about trying to postpone the meeting but realized it was too late to do so. He could still get the information he needed and arrive at the meeting on time if he worked rapidly. He turned to the computer again when the phone rang. "Auto Claims. Atkins speaking," Carl said brusquely.

Angela Carter is a teller at a suburban branch office of a bank. She often goes out to dinner with some of her co-workers on Mondays. While driving home from one such dinner in the rain, Angela stopped for a red light. She became fearful when her eyes were drawn to the rearview mirror by reflected head lights. A car approaching behind her showed no sign of slowing down. Although she was wearing a seatbelt, Angela was severely jostled when the other car hit hers from the rear.

Sam Unger, the driver of the other car, rushed to help Angela out of her car and to see whether she was all right. Angela didn't seem injured, so they began to look at the damage to their vehicles. Angela's left rear light was broken, and her rear bumper was dented. Sam Unger's car showed little sign of damage. It was clear to both of them that Sam had skidded on wet leaves when he had applied the brakes. Perhaps he was also traveling too fast given the rainy conditions.

Angela and Sam agreed that they were fortunate that they had not been hurt and that the damage was not more severe. They exchanged names, addresses, phone numbers, and insurance information. The police were not called to the scene of the accident. Both Angela and Sam were able to drive their vehicles home.

At home, Angela phoned her insurance agent to report the accident. Since it was after normal business hours, she reached an answering machine and left a message. The agent returned her call that night, listened to Angela's description of the accident, and asked a couple of questions, including the name of Sam Unger's insurance company,

Insure-All. The agent urged Angela to go to an emergency room to be examined by a physician. He also explained that the cost of repairing her vehicle should be paid by Sam Unger's insurer. Angela only had liability insurance and that did not cover damage to her vehicle. "Get in touch with them right away. And stay after them," the agent advised. "Don't let them wear you down."

The next morning, Angela felt fine. She decided she didn't need to go to the hospital but she did want to have her car repaired. She drove to work and told the friends she had had dinner with the night before about the accident. "Take your agent's advice," one of them said. "Call the insurance company right away."

Angela decided to do that. She dug out the information Sam Unger had given her and called Insure-All's offices. A recorded voice gave Angela a number of options. She was told to press 3 to report a claim, and she did so. After several moments, a recorded voice said they were interested in her call and she should wait to talk with the next available claim representative. After a few more moments, the recorded voice repeated the message. Angela was about to give up and try calling again later when someone brusquely answered, "Auto Claims. Atkins speaking."

Angela began to describe the accident to Carl Atkins. He interrupted with, "Look. What's your policy number?"

"I don't have a policy with you. I explained I was rear-ended by someone you insure, Sam Unger."

"What's his policy number?"

"I don't know."

"Look. I'm late for a meeting. I can't do anything until I hear from our insured. I'll telephone you later," Carl said and hung up.

Angela listened to the dial tone and thought, "How? You don't even have my number."

She put down the phone and went to tell her co-workers how she had been treated by Insure-All. "Your agent was right, Angela," a co-worker said. "You're going to have to stay after those people. I think you should get a lawyer-and take time off to go to the emergency room. Now."

"Maybe you're right," Angela said. "I feel fine, but I was pretty badly shaken up."

Case Analysis

Analyze this claim report from both an employee performance perspective and from a continuous improvement perspective.

The traditional way (employee performance perspective) would be to find fault with Carl Atkins' performance, perhaps the way his supervisor might at annual review time. From this perspective, these are some factors to consider:

- Carl seems knowledgeable and well-intentioned but less productive than he might be.

- Carl displays poor time management skills.

- Carl does not set clear priorities.

- When Carl is under pressure, his interpersonal skills leave much to be desired.

Carl's performance might be rated below average. He could probably benefit from training in time management and telephone courtesy. Perhaps Carl should not receive an annual salary increase until such time as he has completed mandatory training and his performance can be reevaluated.

Another way to view this same set of case facts, using the continuous improvement perspective, is to consider Carl Atkins as part of processes and systems that to a great extent determine his job performance and over which he has little or no control: Insure-All's process for reporting claims, its telephone system, and its claim-handling process. Examined in this way, Carl's impolite and unhelpful response to Angela is a sign that these processes are not designed to meet the needs of Insure-All's customers.

Carl's apparent lack of interpersonal skills could indicate that Insure-All's claim-reporting process and phone system are designed in such a way that Carl and Insure-All's other claim representatives receive calls that should never reach them because they are in no position to meet the needs of callers. A different system would not have routed Angela's call to Carl. It would have been better, for instance, if she had been asked to record her report so that a claim representative could return her call or to provide her information to a customer service representative who could then initiate the claim process.

Finally, Insure-All's processes appear to be designed to produce "boss satisfaction" rather than "customer satisfaction"; that is, the processes emphasize the needs or desires of supervisors rather than those of customers. Carl's supervisor contributed to Carl's difficulties by insisting he attend an unscheduled meeting with no specific agenda and with no time for preparation even though he stated he needed to prepare for a scheduled meeting with people who could be viewed as customers—a claimant and a claimant's attorney.

[DA02529]

Reputation of the Insurance Business

Jan Carlzon, who established a reputation for his continuous improvement efforts while chief executive officer of SAS, an international airline, coined the term "moments of truth," which has proven useful to students of continuous improvement. A moment of truth occurs every time a customer makes contact with an organization, and an organization's reputation rests to a large extent on the collective experiences of customers during moments of truth.

[DA02530]

CHARACTERISTICS OF THE INSURANCE PRODUCT

Insurance products differ from many other types of consumer products because of certain product-specific qualities. For instance, an individual cannot physically hold the conceptual benefits of an insurance policy—the "insurance promise" to pay claims at the time of a covered loss—unlike a consumer who can experience using tangible features in purchasing an item such as a car, an appliance, or clothing.

Insurance products possess several characteristics that, in combination, make them unusual compared with other products with which consumers are familiar. These are characteristics of the insurance product:

Intangibility

The absence of physical characteristics. For continuous improvement efforts, it underscores the difficulty of measuring or quantifying service.

- Intangibility
- The complexity and legal status of the insurance contract
- The circumstances associated with insurance

The **intangibility** of the insurance product relates to the concept that although purchasers of insurance receive a physical object, the policy, that physical object is not what they purchase. They in fact purchase a promise that an insurer will perform in a specific way if certain conditions should occur in the future. Thus, what purchasers buy is intangible—it cannot be touched, tasted, seen, smelled, or heard. It cannot be used or evaluated at the time of purchase. This intangibility of the insurance product makes it unusual if not unique in the experience of most purchasers. Consumers are urged to squeeze fruit, try on clothes, and test drive cars. The nature of the insurance product forces consumers to go against lifelong habits and traditionally sound advice.

Consider how the intangibility of the insurance product could increase the likelihood that the claim service a claimant (as opposed to the insured) receives from an insurance company could be less than satisfactory. Not only is the insurance product intangible, but in this case the claimant must rely on an intangible product purchased by someone else – the insured policyholder. This characteristic of intangibility distinguishes the insurance product from other consumer products.

Another characteristic of the insurance product is its complexity and legal status: the insurance policy is not only a complex document but also a legal contract. Even the most basic types of insurance policies involve terms and ideas that can appear complicated to anyone other than a specialist—causes of loss, liability, and physical damage are examples. Consumers must purchase what they cannot see and may not fully understand.

Insurance policies are contracts, and so consumers often turn to lawyers, the courts, regulators, and legislators—in addition to producers and insurers—if the product does not work satisfactorily. Because insurers and insureds are parties to a contract, the potential for a confrontation between them is greater than in many other consumer transactions. For example, an auto accident claimant might not understand information or questions using complex or confusing terminology, such as, "You have liability coverage only," or "Do you have our insured's policy number?" Consequently, claimants and insureds alike sometimes hire attorneys, a reflection of the legal status of the insurance product.

Lastly, the circumstances associated with insurance and when its product benefits are used become most apparent at the time of a loss or when dealing with potential losses. Dealing with both circumstances can be unpleasant at best or associated with suffering and tragedy at worst. These associations heighten the emotional level involved in many insurance transactions, thus increasing the difficulty of providing satisfaction through those transactions. For example, the only reason a claimant contacts another individual's insurance company is because the claimant has experienced a loss. The circumstances of losses are sometimes frightening and potentially life-threatening. A claimant's heightened emotional state can place additional pressures on the need for an insurer to provide quality customer service.

THE BENEFITS OF INSURANCE

Insurance has many customer benefits, including the payment of claims and the reduction of uncertainty. However, it is difficult for consumers to understand and experience the benefits of insurance when comparing them with other consumer products.

Some insurance consumers experience a benefit at the time of a loss, while others who do not file a claim might not believe they experience a benefit. These are the benefits of insurance:

- Payment for losses
- Reduction of uncertainty
- Loss control
- Efficient use of resources
- Support for credit
- Reduction of social burdens
- Satisfaction of legal and business requirements
- Source of investment funds

The primary benefit, or role, of insurance is to indemnify individuals, families, and businesses by paying for covered losses.

Because insurance indemnifies covered parties, it reduces the uncertainty created by many loss exposures—for example the death of a family's breadwinner or the destruction of its home. Insurance companies often recommend loss control practices that can help policyholders to prevent some losses or to reduce the financial consequences of losses that do occur. Loss control generally reduces the amount of money insurers must pay in claims, thereby reducing insurance costs to consumers.

Insurance promotes efficient use of resources by making it unnecessary for customers to set aside large amounts of money to pay for the financial consequences of potential future losses. Money that might otherwise be set aside to pay for possible losses can be used to make home improvements or to contribute to the growth of a business.

Insurance provides support for credit so that it is possible for individuals and businesses to obtain loans—guaranteeing that the lender will be paid if the collateral for the loan (such as a house) is destroyed or damaged by an insured event.

Insurance helps to reduce social burdens by providing compensation to injured people. Otherwise, uncompensated accident victims can be a serious financial burden to society.

Insurance is often used to satisfy legal and business requirements. For example, many states require automobile owners to maintain liability insurance coverages. Building contractors are usually required to provide proof of insurance before a construction contract is granted.

Insurance also provides a source for investment funds because insurance companies usually do not immediately need the premiums they collect to pay losses. They often loan some of these funds to businesses. Investment funds promote economic growth and job creation.

While insurance provides all of these benefits, many insurance customers do not experience the benefits of insurance. For example, the reduction of uncertainty provided by insurance is not so much experienced as taken for granted. Furthermore, insurance is based on a pooling and sharing of the financial burden of potential losses. Individuals do not personally experience the benefits that insurance provides to others.

The effect of this inability to experience insurance's intangible benefits is that most consumers reduce the many benefits of insurance to a single benefit—the payment of losses. It is not that all of the other benefits of insurance do not exist or that a case could not be made that insurance is a bargain because of the other benefits; rather, those benefits have little impact and that case will remain unpersuasive because of the inability of consumers to experience those benefits personally. See the exhibit "How Consumers Experience Insurance."

How Consumers Experience Insurance

When the media report on consumers and their experiences with insurance, they typically cite the high premiums spent annually per household or business to maintain appropriate or required insurance coverages. At the same time, the reports give examples of instances in which, although significant sums are spent for coverage, many consumers do not "collect" on their insurance policies. Therefore, on those occasions when insureds do file claims, they expect the claims to be covered and fully paid.

However, the media often do not report that although households and businesses often pay premiums that are perceived as excessive, insurers pay out a significant percentage of every premium dollar collected to insureds and claimants. Rather than illustrating the many intangible benefits of insurance, the media describe insurance as an expensive product that is rarely used and does not provide a value commensurate to its cost when it is used. When the media cite the only benefit of insurance as the payment of losses, they minimize the value of that lone benefit.

The typical media reports on consumers and insurance merely reflect what many customers actually experience. Often, consumers who do not experience all the benefits of insurance personally do not realize their significance and value.

INSURANCE AS A SERVICE

Although insurance companies frequently use the term "products" to refer to the coverages they provide, such as commercial insurance products or homeowners products, insurance should be viewed as a service from a customer satisfaction perspective.

The nature of insurance benefits and the increasing competition to develop and maintain satisfied customers reflect the need for insurance professionals to consider the service aspects of insurance as well as the need for insurers' continuous service quality improvement.

The characteristics and benefits of the insurance product highlight the unique nature of the insurance business. The benefits of insurance are intangible unless a covered loss occurs, but insurance pays for such a loss, reducing the uncertainty of an individual, a family, or a business. The promise of insurance is delivered through a complex legal contract that an insured may ask an insurance professional to clarify, especially during the emotionally difficult time of a loss. When one considers the need for customer satisfaction in the insurance transaction, it becomes apparent that the insurance business should be classed as a service. Service businesses face many customer satisfaction challenges that insurers also must address to remain competitive.

In their book *Service America!*, business experts Karl Albrecht and Ron Zemke cite these ten characteristics that are specific to services:[1]

1. Service is produced at the instant of delivery and cannot be created in advance and stored in inventory.
2. Service cannot be centrally produced, inspected, and stockpiled.
3. Service cannot be demonstrated in advance, nor can a sample be sent in advance for approval.
4. In the absence of a tangible product, customers value service on the basis of their own personal experience.
5. The service experience cannot be resold or transferred to a third party.
6. Faulty service cannot be recalled.
7. Delivery of service usually requires human interaction.
8. Quality assurance is required before production.
9. Customers' assessments of service quality are subjective and strongly influenced by expectations.
10. Customers' assessments of service quality tend to decrease in proportion to the number of employees they encounter during the delivery of service.

All ten of these characteristics apply to insurance business transactions. The performance of the promise contained in an insurance policy, for instance, is produced at the instant of delivery, cannot be sampled in advance, cannot be recalled, and requires human interaction. Thus, it is helpful to recognize insurance as a service and to approach customer satisfaction from that point of view.

Recognizing insurance as a service means that insurance can and will be compared with other services rather than products—with a restaurant meal or a stay in a hotel rather than with the purchase of a sweater or a car. Such a comparison makes clear what a difficult task the insurance business faces in trying to achieve customer satisfaction. The distance in time between the payment for the service and its delivery, the complexity and legal status of the insurance contract, and the unpleasant circumstances associated with insurance are obstacles to customer satisfaction that many service businesses simply do not face. Many services are related to entertainment, leisure, and pleasure rather than loss or misfortune. See the exhibit "Continuous Improvement and Insurance."

Continuous Improvement and Insurance

Insurance organizations are now trying to change the way they do business for reasons ranging from an internal desire to improve to economic pressures that can make change necessary for survival. No matter what the motivation, most of these organizations are trying to become capable of ensuring continuous improvement. This means they are trying to satisfy customers every time a connection or transaction is made. Since customer expectations are shaped by experience, customers will not remain satisfied. Instead, as they become accustomed to a high level of service, their expectations will increase. Continuous improvement is an organizational response to constantly increasing customer expectations.

Continuous improvement is a way for insurance organizations to attract and retain customers, improve the reputation of the organization, improve the reputation of the insurance business, and cause the insurance mechanism to work efficiently, with as little friction as possible. Continuous improvement is based on a new, strategic definition of "quality." In this context, *quality* means *providing goods and services that completely satisfy both internal and external customers by meeting their explicit and implicit expectations.* Organizations engage in continuous improvement by becoming customer-oriented, improving processes, and involving employees.

[DA04416]

SUMMARY

Organizations today are changing the way they do business because of the need to improve the organization and respond to a changing external environment. These organizational changes focus on quality and continuous improvement.

The insurance product has several characteristics that distinguish it from other products with which consumers are familiar. These characteristics are intangibility, the complexity and legal status of the insurance contract, and the circumstances associated with insurance.

These are the benefits of insurance:

- Payment for losses
- Reduction of uncertainty
- Loss control
- Efficient use of resources
- Support for credit
- Reduction of social burdens
- Satisfaction of legal and business requirements

However, consumers are not able to experience the benefits of insurance in the same way that they experience the benefits of other consumer products.

The characteristics of the insurance product and the way consumers experience many of the benefits of insurance indicate that insurance should be classed as a service. Services face some specific challenges to the delivery of quality; that is, providing goods and services that completely satisfy both internal and external customers by meeting their explicit and implicit expectations.

ASSIGNMENT NOTE

1. Karl Albrecht and Ron Zemke, Service America! Doing Business in the New Economy (Homewood, Ill.: Dow Jones-Irwin, 1985), pp. 36-37.

2

Customer Identification

Educational Objectives

After learning the content of this assignment, you should be able to:

▷ Describe a work process.

▷ Describe one or more outputs of a given work process.

▷ Identify the types of customers in a given process.

Customer Identification

2

WORK PROCESSES

Providing goods and services to customers through work processes fulfills the wants and needs of those customers.

Continuous improvement consists of three fundamental elements—customer orientation, process improvement, and employee involvement. Here we deal with customer orientation and customer identification by examining a manufacturing **work process** and a service work process.

Orientation is a way of gaining a sense of direction by reference to a landmark. The word seems to have originally meant to face the rising sun and thus identify the east. Using the sun as a landmark provided a sense of direction. Customer orientation means gaining a sense of direction for an organization by frequent and repeated reference to customers as landmarks. Because customers are multiple and various, using them as landmarks is complex. The first step in acquiring a customer orientation is identifying **customers**.

Manufacturing Work Process

Continuous improvement is basically about work. Work is a process, a sequence of specific steps. Looking at work as a process shows that the current continuous improvement movement, or Quality Revolution, has a long history. It began with the industrial quality control efforts of manufacturing firms.

Industrial quality control included determining clear specifications for products before producing them and then inspecting some or all of the products to confirm that they conformed to the specifications before shipping them to customers. In general terms, the manufacturing work process can be depicted as a work group initiating the work process from raw materials with the output going to the customer. See the exhibit "Manufacturing Work Process."

This manufacturing work process can be said to have a "product orientation" because it is based on four assumptions:

- The manufacturer knows what the product should be.
- The manufacturer can measure the product.
- The manufacturer can determine whether the product meets the specifications within acceptable limits.
- Customers will be satisfied with products that meet specifications.

Work process
A sequence of steps designed to produce a specific product or provide a specific service.

Customer
A person who receives outputs.

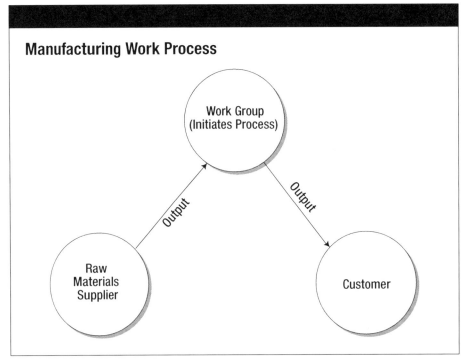

Manufacturing Work Process

[DA04418]

In short, quality was defined by manufacturers as conformance to specifications.

A product orientation results in an internal orientation for the firm. If products fail to conform to specifications, the management of the firm will look to its combination of raw materials, employees, and equipment to solve the problem. Product orientation also implies an attitude toward sales. Ralph Waldo Emerson famously summed up that attitude in the nineteenth century with the phrase, "If you build a better mousetrap, the world will beat a path to your door." Emerson naturally assumed that the makers of mousetraps knew or could determine the specifications of a better mousetrap. There was no need to define "better." What better means would be obvious to a mousetrap manufacturer.

Service Work Process

Customer orientation

Occurs when an organization looks toward its customers and responds to them.

Engaging in work processes that result in services, rather than products, necessitates a **customer orientation**. Customers know what the service experience should be. Customers help service providers translate their expectations into measurable specifications. Customers determine whether the service meets specifications, that is, satisfies their expectations. In short, quality means meeting or exceeding customer expectations.

A customer orientation implies an external focus for an organization. If a service fails to meet customer expectations, the management of the organization will look to customers—rather than to the combination of raw materials, employees, and equipment—for a solution to the problem. Customer orientation also implies an attitude toward sales. That attitude has been described by Philip Kotler, in his book *Marketing Management*, as the **marketing approach**, that is, the assumption that an organization's objectives can best be achieved through the complete satisfaction of the end user—the customer.[1]

Marketing approach

Assumes that an organization's objectives can best be met by completely satisfying the end user.

First, the customer's requirements or expectations, rather than the manufacturer's specifications, initiate the process. Second, although the service provider, or work group, might rely on a supplier, the supplier is sought out and selected based on the work group's requirements, which are a reflection of the customer's requirements. Indeed, the work group is the supplier's customer. Third, this process does not end with the delivery of the service to the customer. On the contrary, the work group solicits feedback from the customer and provides feedback to the supplier. A diagram of a service work process shows the customer, the work group, and the supplier with the requirements, output, and feedback between the three entities. See the exhibit "Service Work Process."

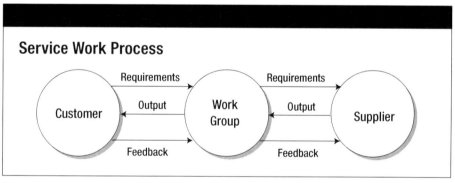

Service Work Process

[DA04419]

The service work process is continuous. Allowing the customer to determine requirements for satisfaction before delivery and seeking feedback from the customer after service has been delivered means that the service work process is designed to ensure improvement. The service work process is fundamental to the idea of continuous improvement. Because of the influence of advocates of continuous improvement, both manufacturing and service organizations now take this approach, determining requirements by establishing customer expectations. See the exhibit "A Page From the History of Quality."

The service work process helps to provide answers to a key question: Who are customers? The answers to that question depend on where the person providing the answers appears in the work process. The shortest answer to the question is "whoever receives your output." The following example might help clarify that answer.

Roger Pennypacker, an insurance agent, has obtained permission to quote on property insurance on an apartment house. Elfrieda Albright owns the apart-

A Page From the History of Quality

W. Edwards Deming is known as the person responsible for Japan's transformation into an industrial success following World War II. Armed with a PhD in mathematical physics from Yale University (1927), Deming became a teacher of mathematics and statistics at the United States Department of Agriculture (USDA). There, he became familiar with the work of Walter Shewhart, who developed the approach of using of statistical analysis in relation to quality control. Deming later applied statistical analysis methods to clerical work at the Bureau of the Census.

When World War II ended, Deming conducted a study of the war's effects on Japan's agricultural production. His meetings with statisticians and business leaders in Japan led him to believe that his statistical methods could help Japan become a leading producer of quality products. Returning to Japan in 1950 to teach his methods to members of the Union of Japanese Scientists and Engineers (JUSE), he predicted that the quality of Japanese products would capture world markets within five years; his prediction came true in four years. In appreciation for his work, the JUSE in 1951 established the Deming Prize, which continues to be awarded in recognition of quality production.

Deming turned his attention to the United States, teaching his methods for the next forty years. Many of the people he taught later became leaders of American businesses.

His main interest was in helping people reach their full potential. A profile of Deming at the American Society for Quality Web site describes Deming's philosophy based on his avocation as an organist and composer: "His version of the National Anthem, which addresses people's inability to hit all the notes, serves as a metaphor for one of his points of management: Don't blame the singers (workers) if the song is written poorly (the system is the problem); instead, rewrite the music (fix the system). In life and art, Deming simply wanted to make it easier for people to sing."

American Society for Quality, "W. Edwards Deming, A mission pursued on two continents," http://asq.org/about-asq/who-we-are/bio_deming.html (accessed September 9, 2011). [DA04420]

ment house and is a prospective new client for Pennypacker. Pennypacker inspects the premises and interviews Elfrieda in an attempt to understand her insurance needs. Once he has gathered this information, he turns the material over to the staff of the Pennypacker Agency to complete applications for insurance and to solicit quotations from four or five of the insurance companies the agency represents.

Who is the customer in this scenario? The obvious answer is Elfrieda Albright. But is she the only one?

This scenario describes the first phase of the service work process—learning requirements and submitting information to a supplier. A diagram can show the first phase of the service work process. By looking at a service work process, it is possible to say that Elfrieda Albright is the customer and Pennypacker is the work group (a group of one, in this case). See the exhibit "Requirements in the Service Work Process."

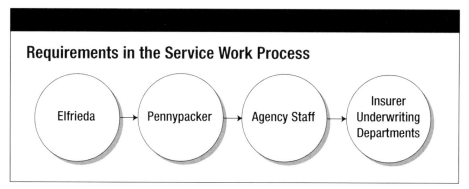

Requirements in the Service Work Process

Elfrieda → Pennypacker → Agency Staff → Insurer Underwriting Departments

[DA04425]

Elfrieda tells Pennypacker of her insurance needs in her own way. He inspects the premises and listens to Elfrieda but explains what her needs are, based on his knowledge of insurance; current market conditions; the desires, preferences, and requirements of the underwriting departments of the companies he represents; and so on. The agency staff is a work group, and Pennypacker is its supplier. Since work groups are the customers of suppliers, the agency staff is now Pennypacker's customer. The process does not end there.

If a customer is defined as anyone who receives an output, the underwriters are the customers of the agency staff. The underwriters are customers when they receive the output from the agency—the completed applications for insurance and other information. The underwriters perform a work process, become a work group when they underwrite the applications, deciding whether to accept them and, if so, at what prices and under what conditions.

TYPES OF OUTPUTS

Products or services as outputs can be supplied to satisfy wants and need of customers.

An output is any product or service that results from a work process. A work process is a sequence of steps designed to produce a specific product or provide a specific service. Outputs that are services are very different from outputs that are products.

A mousetrap represents the output of a work process. A mousetrap is an output that is a product. Advocates of continuous improvement distinguish outputs that are products by three characteristics: (1) customers are not involved in the production of the product; (2) the product is tangible—it can be inspected, measured, tested, perhaps tasted, and so on; and (3) repetitive processes are used to produce the product.

Issuing an insurance policy is an example of a work process that results in an output that is a product. An insurance policy is a tangible product. (The policy itself is a tangible product. The promise to perform contained in the policy is intangible.) Customers are not involved in the production of the insurance policy. The process of issuing insurance policies is a repetitive one. Specifications for an insurance policy can be determined in advance. For instance, the information contained in the policy must be complete and accurate. Determining whether these specifications have been met can be confirmed by inspection of the policy before mailing it to the customer. If these specifications are not met, the management of the firm or the supervisor of the policy issuance group will look internally to solve the problem.

Customers are involved in the production of services. This involvement of customers is called coproduction. The output is intangible. The work process that results in the output is a **nonrepetitive work process**; it takes place once and cannot be repeated. It is at least arguable that the work process that results in a service is unique.

Settling an insurance claim is an example of a work process that results in an output that is a service. Customers are involved in settling the claim; that is, coproduction is necessary to the transaction. The output is intangible—it cannot be inspected, tested, tasted, sniffed, and so on. The work process that results in the output certainly has some repetitive aspects, but most claim representatives would agree that every claim is different. Quality is not determined by conforming to specifications but by the reaction of the claimant, the customer. This customer reaction is called the outcome, a stage beyond the output.

Outputs in the service work process are considered outputs rather than requirements. It indicates that the staff of the Pennypacker Agency is a customer of the underwriting departments of the insurers represented by the agency. The agency staff receives the output of the underwriters, the quotations or declinations. At that point, the agency staff are the customers of the underwriters. See the exhibit "Outputs in the Service Work Process."

Nonrepetitive work process

A sequence of specific steps that produces an output and varies each time it is performed.

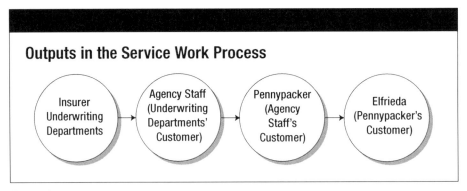

[DA04427]

Once the agency's staff obtains the quotations and prepares a proposal for writing the business for property insurance on an apartment house, insurance agent Roger Pennypacker schedules a meeting with apartment house owner Elfrieda Albright to give her the proposal, explain it, and attempt to close the deal. Pennypacker is then the staff's customer, and Elfrieda is Pennypacker's customer.

This means that it is not always clear who the customers are. Even a routine transaction when diagrammed and analyzed can become relatively complex, and the roles of the people involved in the process change at various stages of the process. This is, in part, because there is more than one type of customer.

TYPES OF CUSTOMERS

The first step in acquiring a customer orientation is identifying customers.

One of the obstacles to continuous improvement in insurance is the business's tendency to avoid the word "customers," using instead "risks" or "policyholders," perhaps a reflection on how customers have traditionally been viewed—that is, as potential losses.

One of the basic ideas of continuous improvement is that everyone who is involved in a work process has customers—**internal customers, external customers**, or **end users** (ultimate customers).

Defining a customer as the person who receives an output is advantageous for three reasons:

- It is specific. General statements about customers—"XYZ Communications is one of our biggest customers" or "Fly-By-Night Airlines is one of our worst customers"—are vague.

- It is personal. Thinking of organizations rather than of individuals as customers decreases the usefulness of customer identification. In fact, it is likely that the risk manager of XYZ Communications is one of the organization's biggest customers, and the treasurer of Fly-By-Night Airlines is one of the organization's worst customers. The answer to the question of who is the customer should be the name of an individual.

- Defining a customer as the person who receives your output de-emphasizes the organization for which that individual works. This definition of a customer allows for both internal and external customers.

External customer
A person from outside of the organization who receives outputs.

Internal customer
A person who receives outputs from a work group within the same organization.

End user
An ultimate customer, the user of the final product or service.

Internal Customers

Consider what Roger Pennypacker needs to do to obtain quotes on property insurance for Elfrieda Albright's apartment building. After he interviewed Elfrieda and inspected the premises, he submitted material to the staff of his agency. His notes, photographs, recommendations, and suggestions all constitute an output received by the staff. At that point, Pennypacker's staff is his customer. For that reason, he should be specific (he will provide the material to the office manager), he should be personal (he will provide the material to Oloona MacNamara), and he should ignore the fact that he and Oloona work for the same organization. It is indeed likely that Oloona works for Roger. That does not matter. What matters is that Oloona receives Pennypacker's output and therefore she is his customer. He should be aware of her requirements and set out to meet or exceed her expectations. Oloona MacNamara should be treated as a customer by Pennypacker even though she is an internal customer.

Why? Is this a call for revolution in the workplace and a reversal of roles? Should bosses go around trying to meet or exceed the needs of their employees because doing so would make America's offices kinder, gentler places? No—or, at least, not exactly. The reason is that it is impossible to meet the needs of end users without meeting the needs of every customer, internal or external, who is part of a work process.

External Customers

Similarly, Oloona MacNamara should be specific about her customers— the underwriting departments who will receive the applications for insurance and additional information from Oloona (the underwriting departments of Insure-All, Risk Free Insurance, Professional Fire and Casualty, and Realtors Mutual). She should be personal about the underwriters, underwriting managers, or branch managers who will receive her output (Megan Kemp at Insure-All, Will Gleason at Risk Free, Joan Deming at PF&C, and Rodney Evans at Realtors).

Finally, she should ignore the fact that these individuals are not employed by the Pennypacker Agency and seek to understand their requirements, needs, and expectations because they are her external customers. Only through these underwriters can Oloona meet the needs of her primary customer, Roger Pennypacker, when he receives her output of the proposal, and, through him, Elfrieda Albright, the end user of the proposal.

End Users

Customer orientation implies the attitude toward sales that Philip Kotler describes as "the marketing approach," that is, the assumption that an organization can best achieve its objectives through the complete satisfaction of the end user—the ultimate customer.[2] This identification of the customer with the end user recognizes how difficult it can be to identify customers and acknowledges the need to be specific when referring to customers.

Many, in fact most, people do not directly encounter end users. The only way for such people to be customer oriented is to identify and focus attention on those internal and external customers whom they do encounter, those internal and external customers who receive the outputs they produce.

Service work processes combine and overlap to make what are sometimes long and complex delivery chains. This fact adds to the difficulty of satisfying customers in service businesses such as insurance. Customer orientation requires that these long and complex chains be broken down, diagrammed, and analyzed so that all internal and external customers are specifically, personally, and clearly identified.

The way to identify them is to track outputs and determine who receives them. This approach clears away a lot of gunk—office politics, positions of power and authority, practices that continue out of inertia, habit, or tradition, and so on—that clogs up a system to reveal how it really works. Identifying customers in this way is an important first step toward the customer orientation that continuous improvement demands.

SUMMARY

A work process is a sequence of specific steps that produces an output. Work processes have evolved from those established by manufacturers into those that represent the approach taken by service businesses. This evolution represents a shift from a product orientation and an internal focus to a customer orientation and an external focus. This shift reflects the changing nature of outputs.

An output is any product or service that results from a work process. Outputs that are services typically involve coproduction (customer involvement), are intangible, and result from processes that are nonrepetitive. This evolution also represents a shift from sales to the marketing approach, that is, the assumption that an organization can best achieve its objectives through the complete satisfaction of the ultimate customer, the end user.

Customers, or people who receive outputs, should be identified personally, because it is specific, it is personal, and it de-emphasizes the organization. Customers can be identified as internal customers, external customers, or end users.

ASSIGNMENT NOTES

1.   Philip Kotler, Marketing Management (Englewood Cliffs, N.J.: Prentice-Hall, 1984), pp. 17-29.

2.   Philip Kotler, Marketing Management (Englewood Cliffs, N.J.: Prentice-Hall, 1984).

Direct Your Learning ▶▶

3

What Customers Want

Educational Objectives

After learning the content of this assignment, you should be able to:

▶ Describe the strategic definition of quality.

▶ Describe the following measures of quality: (a) work process measures, (b) output measures (including distinguishing between the voice of the process and the voice of the customer), and (c) outcome measures.

▶ Apply work process measures, output measures, and outcome measures to the analysis of an insurance function or operation.

▶ Describe the customer expectations reflected in the phrase "faster, better, cheaper."

▶ Describe the eight dimensions of quality.

▶ Summarize the RATER criteria.

▶ Distinguish among the following levels of expectations: (a) implicit customer expectations, (b) explicit expectations, and (c) latent expectations.

What Customers Want

3

QUALITY STRATEGICALLY DEFINED

Continuous improvement requires the need to determine what customers want.

An understanding of the definition of **quality** is necessary before considering the three levels of quality measures—work process measures, output measures, and outcome measures. These three levels of measurement are important for an understanding of what customers want.

Continuous improvement is based on a strategic definition of quality, that is, a definition that helps organizations decide what to do and how to do it. Simply put, the strategic definition of quality is to meet or exceed the needs of customers. If quality means meeting the needs of customers, identifying customers and determining their needs are two prerequisites to quality. Many continuous improvement advocates have restated the strategic definition of quality as an operating objective. That objective calls for the continuous improvement of every output, whether a product or a service, through the removal of unwanted variation and by improving work processes.

The continuous improvement operating objective concentrates on work processes and outputs in order to ensure quality. Three key ingredients to what customers want include quality measures, quality criteria, and levels of expectations.

Quality Measurement

Quality, especially in service businesses, is subjective and based on expectations. Organizations that wish to ensure customer satisfaction must try to translate the subjective into the objective, to find a way to measure their performance. Continuous improvement advocates have found that this can best be accomplished by measuring performance on three levels—the work process level, the output level, and the outcome level.

Quality Criteria

Although quality is always in the eye of the customer (that is, it has been strategically defined as meeting the needs of customers), the two types of outputs meet those needs in different ways. For products, quality is achieved through the characteristics of the product. For services, quality is achieved through the characteristics of employees of the service provider. Most organizations must

Quality
To meet or exceed customers' needs.

concentrate on meeting the needs of customers through both products and services.

Levels of Expectations

While it is true that it is easier to measure the characteristics of a product than those of a service, both can be measured and in similar ways. The strategic definition of quality is responsible for the similarity of these methods. If quality resides in the satisfaction of the customer, the responses of customers, as well as the characteristics of products or services, must be studied and measured.

QUALITY MEASUREMENT

The quality of goods and services are important to customers.

Output measures

Measures that apply to specific characteristics, features, or attributes of a product or service.

Work process measures

Apply to the activities and operations that produce output. They establish targets for operations and help coordinate employees, equipment, and material.

Outcome measures

Measures that apply to the effect of the output on the customer and how the customer uses the product or services.

The three levels of quality measures are **work process measures, output measures**, and **outcome measures**. These three levels of measurement are important for an understanding of what customers want and are important in the study of process improvement. The voice of the process and the voice of the customer, two points of view with regard to output measures, are fundamental concepts.

Work Process Measures

Work process measures apply to the activities and operations that produce outputs. They establish measurable targets for functions and provide a way to coordinate people, equipment, and material. The purpose of these measures is to help predict the characteristics of outputs.

Output Measures

Output measures apply to specific characteristics, features, or attributes of a product or service. They are developed from two points of view—the point of view of the process and the point of view of the customer—and then the two points of view are compared.

Voice of the process

The output measures that describe actual outputs and capabilities of the process.

Voice of the customer

The output measures that describe customers' needs, wants, and expectations.

Output measures developed from the process point of view describe actual outputs and imply what the process is capable of producing. These output measures are called the **voice of the process**. Output measures developed from the customer point of view describe outputs the customer wants and imply what customers need or expect. These output measures are called the **voice of the customer**.

Outcome Measures

Outcome measures apply to the effect of the output on the customer. They depend on what the customer does with the output, no matter whether it is a product or a service. The outcome level is the most important level of performance measurement, but it is the most difficult to grasp and use because it is highly influenced by the customer's work process. For this reason, outcome measures cannot be determined before delivery of the product or service.

All three levels of measurement are necessary and should be coordinated. But since outcome measures are most directly related to customer satisfaction, they are the most important. Process measures and output measures should be aligned to achieve satisfactory performance at the outcome level.

QUALITY MEASUREMENT APPLICATIONS

The quality of services supplied by an insurer is important to customers (insureds).

The three levels of quality measures are work process measures, output measures, and outcome measures. These measures apply in manufacturing and other forms of business, such as insurance. These three levels of measurement are important for an understanding of what customers want and are important in the study of process improvement. The voice of the process (performed by an insurer) and the voice of the customer (or insured), two points of view with regard to output measures, are fundamental concepts in an insurance transaction.

Work Process Measures in Insurance

An insurance company could have a standard operating procedure that states that policies must be issued within two working days of receipt of all required information. This operating procedure provides two kinds of work process measures. First, it sets a time limit for acceptable performance by the policy issuance group—all policies are to be issued within two working days. Second, it establishes "supplier requirements" for underwriters and others who provide the policy issuance group with information—all required information must be received by the policy issuance group before policies will be processed.

These two work process measures make it possible to predict two characteristics of the outputs, the issued policies. First, policies will contain all of the required information. Second, policies will be processed in no more than two working days. If the work process measures are met, these output characteristics will be consistently achieved without a need to inspect the outputs.

Output Measures in Insurance

In the work process measures example, the policies will be issued within two working days of receipt by the issuance group of all the required information. From the process point of view, that two-day turnaround can be an acceptable standard consistently achieved. From the customer point of view, however, the variation in the amount of time it takes the company to issue a policy can be extreme and consistently below expectations.

From the point of view of the customer, the time taken to gather and provide complete information to the policy issuance group is part of the process. Customers could wait weeks or even months for their policies even though the policy issuance group consistently meets its process measure of a two-day turnaround. In this case, there is a gap between the voice of the process, that is, what the process actually delivers, and the voice of the customer, that is, what the customer actually needs or expects.

Outcome Measures in Insurance

Many personal lines insurance purchasers might put their auto and homeowners insurance policies in a safe place after receiving them without even reading them. All they want to do with them, in effect, is to keep them as a proof of purchase. For such customers, when they receive the policies might not matter a great deal. They will be satisfied if the policy arrives within a reasonable amount of time after they have paid the premium.

A risk manager for a large chemical manufacturing firm, on the other hand, might need the insurance policies to do other things—provide copies to the accounting and legal departments, prepare for a quarterly meeting of a corporate safety committee, or meet with the heads of manufacturing departments and the human resources department to develop and implement a training program that will fulfill a loss control procedure required by a workers compensation underwriter.

Clearly, in this case, when the policies are received is crucial for the work process of the risk manager. An unanticipated delay in the delivery of a policy could not only cause scheduling problems for the risk manager but could also keep the chemical manufacturer from complying with a condition of coverage stipulated by an underwriter—implementation of the underwriter's required loss control procedure.

FASTER, BETTER, CHEAPER

Suppliers need to determine what customers want.

Researchers have determined criteria that reflect what customers want. Generally, customers want products that are faster, better, and cheaper.

Quality criteria are based on the fact that customers pay for products and services. Satisfaction with products and services is therefore related to a sense of value. The relationship between price and value is complex and for the purposes of this course can be left to the economists. Oscar Wilde once suggested the difference between price and value by defining a cynic as someone who "knows the price of everything and the value of nothing."

It is enough to recognize that the price paid by a customer is one of the elements that helps determine whether the customer considers the purchase a fair exchange. Customers are unlikely to be satisfied with products and services they obtain through what they consider to be unfair exchanges. Still, price is only one of three elements that determine a customer's response to a product or service. Time and quality are the other two elements.

In general, customers are satisfied when they purchase products or services that are "faster, better, and cheaper" than those available elsewhere. "Cheaper" relates to price. "Faster" relates to time and can be translated into "convenience"—the availability of the product or service and the ease and speed with which the customer can conduct the transaction. With direct mail advertising (one of the ways in which insurance is distributed), the phrase "Send no money now" significantly increases the number of responses. In part, this increased response to the ads is based on convenience: customers can conduct the transaction "faster" than they could if they needed, for instance, to write and include a check with their response.

Price and convenience, however, do not exhaust the elements of "value," of the customer's sense that the transaction represents a fair exchange. "Better," which translates into quality, is the third element. Even a low-priced, readily accessible product or service will cause customer dissatisfaction, the sense that the transaction represents an unfair exchange, if the product or service fails to meet the needs of customers.

Although "better" is, of course, the vaguest and the most difficult to measure of these three elements, it is the most important because it is an outcome measure; it depends on what the customer does with the output.

For example, a chemical manufacturing firm's risk manager who relies on receipt of insurance policies to do his job is in a position to choose among insurance providers. If one of these providers not only meets the price and convenience considerations of the competition but also personally delivers the policies to the risk manager, reviews them, answers questions about them, and offers suggestions the risk manager can use at the corporate safety committee meeting and can use to develop required loss control training, that provider can be said to "add value" to the transaction and, thus, to deliver quality service. In this case, the satisfaction of the risk manager is not based on price or convenience—they are assumed to be equivalent for all potential providers of insurance—but on "better" service, the quality element of value.

Two of the three primary things customers want—price and convenience—are not only the easiest to measure but also the easiest to understand. "Better"

calls for study and elaboration. "Better" varies for the two types of outputs, products and services.

EIGHT DIMENSIONS OF QUALITY

Quality means to meet or exceed customers' needs.

Developed by David Garvin and presented in a *Harvard Business Review* article, the eight dimensions of quality serve as another set of criteria by which organizations can begin to analyze the characteristics of quality.[1] Focusing primarily on the quality of products, Garvin's dimensions are perhaps most readily applicable to the auto industry. Still, he insisted that they could be adapted to service businesses and they demonstrate again the kinds of things that customers want.

Garvin's eight dimensions of quality are these: (1) performance, (2) features, (3) reliability, (4) conformance, (5) durability, (6) serviceability, (7) aesthetics, and (8) perceived quality.

Garvin wrote, "Managers have to stop thinking about quality merely as a narrow effort to gain control of the production process, and to start thinking more rigorously about consumers' needs and preferences."

Intending, in part, to alert business executives to the changing definition of quality, Garvin promulgated his eight dimensions of quality:

1. Performance refers to a product's primary functional characteristic.
2. Features refers to additional performance characteristics, choices, and options available to a customer.
3. Reliability refers to a product's ability to perform a specific function for a specific time under specific conditions.
4. Conformance refers to the degree to which a product's characteristics meet existing standards.
5. Durability refers to the useful life of a product and is related to both reliability and serviceability. It focuses on the need of customers to compare the potential cost to repair a product with the cost of replacing the product.
6. Serviceability expands the costs of repairing a product to include the inconvenience and temporary loss-of-use of a product that repairs also cause. It focuses on the nonfinancial aspects of the repair experience—the convenience, competence, and courtesy with which repairs are made.
7. Aesthetics refers to the pleasure derived from the tangible characteristics of a product and is the most subjective of the eight dimensions of quality.
8. Perceived quality refers to reputation. Customers frequently have at best incomplete information on products and services. They tend to compare them based on the reported experiences of others.

THE RATER CRITERIA

Researchers have determined criteria that reflect what customers generally want.

A set of criteria for quality was developed with service businesses specifically in mind. These five criteria are called RATER criteria because the first letters of the criteria, when put together, spell "rater," a convenient aid to memory.[2]

The five RATER criteria for quality measurement are these:

1. Reliability—The promised service can be accurately performed by the provider.
2. Assurance—Customers believe and have confidence in the service provider because of the competence and courtesy of employees.
3. Tangibles—The impression made on customers by the service provider's offices, equipment, personnel, and so on is positive.
4. Empathy—The service provider's employees demonstrate concern for customers and give them individual attention.
5. Responsiveness—The service provider's employees are prompt and eager to be of help to customers.

Some insurance companies use these criteria in judging new prospective agencies. See the exhibit "A Page From the History of Quality."

A Page From the History of Quality

Philip B. Crosby, who worked at various manufacturing firms beginning with the Crosley Corporation in 1952, first established a widespread reputation when he served as director of quality on the Pershing missile project at the Martin Marietta Corporation. He was responsible for the "zero-defects" program of that project, a program that not only drastically reduced manufacturing defects but eventually became government policy.

As the vice president of quality at ITT, Crosby began the Quality College as a way to disseminate the concepts and techniques of quality to ITT employees. In 1979, Crosby published his best-selling book, *Quality Is Free*, and retired to Winter Park, Florida, where he established his own consulting firm and the Quality College.

Zero errors, Crosby argued, can and should be a realistic target. Most people would no doubt agree that surgeons, for instance, should strive for zero fatalities, and that airline pilots should strive for zero accidents. Crosby advocates that those involved in other kinds of work should strive for the same standard.

Crosby is also known for his definition of quality as "conformance to requirements, not elegance," a definition that shows his desire to make quality measurable rather than subjective. When others had less success in implementing "zero defects," Crosby attributed the disappointing results to a lack of management commitment, a problem often cited by Juran and Deming as well. Although some of Crosby's ideas have been difficult for others to implement in some settings, he has done a great deal to spread the knowledge of quality concepts and techniques throughout the American business community.

LEVELS OF EXPECTATION

In recent decades, the study of determining what customers want has increased.

One result of the increasing rigor that was brought to the analysis of customer satisfaction is the realization of the three levels of customer expectations. Customer expectations can be described as consisting of a hierarchy of three levels: **implicit expectations**, **explicit expectations**, and **latent expectations**. These various levels of expectations can be summarized. See the exhibit "Customer Expectation Levels."

Explicit customer expectations

Options that customers are aware of and can select.

Implicit customer expectations

Basic requirements that customers often take for granted.

Latent customer expectations

Features that customers did not know existed or were unaware of wanting.

Customer Expectation Levels

Customer Expectations	Effect of Meeting Expectations
Latent expectations (Unaware of existence)	Delight
Explicit expectations (Choices and options)	Satisfaction
Implicit expectations (Taken for granted)	No dissatisfaction

[DA04429]

Implicit Expectations

Implicit expectations refer to those basic requirements that tend to be taken for granted. That a telecommunications system consistently provides callers with a dial tone, that an automobile consistently provides drivers with the ability to make turns without toppling over, and that an insurance company pays claims for covered losses are examples of requirements at the implicit level. Meeting implicit expectations can keep customers from becoming dissatisfied, but it will not cause customers to applaud the quality of a service or product.

Explicit Expectations

Explicit expectations refer to those choices and options that customers are aware of and take an active part in selecting. A telecommunications system that not only consistently provides callers with a dial tone but also offers long distance service, voice mail, and other options is in a position to meet the explicit expectations of customers. An automobile that not only consistently provides drivers with the ability to turn safely but also offers a range of colors, interiors, sunroofs, and security systems addresses the explicit expectations of customers. An insurance company that not only pays claims at the time of loss but also offers customers a range of deductibles, limits of liability, premium payment plans, and loss control services addresses the explicit expectations of customers. Meeting explicit expectations can not only keep customers from becoming dissatisfied but can also actively satisfy them because it means exceeding implicit expectations.

Latent Expectations

Latent expectations refer to characteristics or features that customers did not know to be available or were unaware of wanting. Meeting these expectations can not only satisfy customers but can also delight them because meeting these expectations means exceeding explicit expectations. When latent expectations are met, customers experience "added value," the sense that the transaction provided them with more than they consciously expected. Carmakers seek to delight customers by offering such features as remote starters. Insurance organizations do so by performing annual insurance reviews or offering a policyholder's bill of rights. Determining latent expectations and setting out to meet them is one of the aims of customer orientation.

Satisfying Expectations

The characteristics of a product or service that correspond to the three levels of expectation change over time. When first introduced, alternative premium payment plans in personal lines insurance delighted customers because they offered a convenience few customers consciously wanted, much less expected. As the range of these plans expanded, customers were satisfied because they could choose from among all the options they could possibly expect. Now the full range of alternative premium payment plans is taken for granted by customers. Customers would become dissatisfied if the range of premium payment plans narrowed or disappeared. The ongoing presence of the full range of premium payment plans does not cause customer satisfaction but merely prevents dissatisfaction. This shifting of product or service characteristics through the three-level hierarchy of expectations clarifies the nature of continuous improvement. Keeping up with customers' changing expectations translates into the constant improvement of products and services.

The three levels of expectations also serve as a guide to organizations on how to listen to the voice of the customer. If customers take implicit expectations for granted and are unaware of latent expectations, information on explicit expectations can be most profitably solicited from customers. Focusing on the choices and options customers consciously want can help an organization achieve customer satisfaction and simultaneously learn the nature of latent expectations, the sources of delight for customers.

The relationship between customer expectations and customer loyalty (the ability to retain customers) is clearly evident. It is a reminder that the purpose of an organization's customer orientation is to attract and retain customers.

SUMMARY

One of the reasons for the customer orientation that continuous improvement demands is the need to determine what customers want. This need reflects the strategic definition of quality. That definition states that quality means meeting or exceeding the needs of customers. With this definition in mind, one would find delivering quality service to be possible only when knowing what customers want.

The three levels of quality measurements are work process measures, output measures, and outcome measures. Work process measures deal with the specific procedures that produce an output. Output measures are the characteristics of a product or service from two points of view, the voice of the process and the voice of the customer. Outcome measures apply to the effect of the output on the customer.

In insurance, the three levels of quality measurements are work process measures, output measures, and outcome measures. Work process measures deal with the specific procedures that produce an output. Output measures are the characteristics of a product or service from two points of view, the voice of the process by the insurer and the voice of the customer (or insured). Outcome measures apply to the effect of the output of the insurer on the customer (or insured).

Customers want products or services that are faster, better, and cheaper. Price is one of the considerations because customers seek value and the customer's sense of value is clearly related to price. Faster relates to convenience, the ease and speed with which a product or service can be obtained. Better relates to quality, the most important and the most difficult to determine of the criteria.

David Garvin promulgated the eight dimensions of quality— (1) performance, (2) features, (3) reliability, (4) conformance, (5) durability, (6) serviceability, (7) aesthetics, and (8) perceived quality.

The RATER criteria of quality were developed specifically for service customers. These five criteria are (1) reliability, (2) assurance, (3) tangibles, (4) empathy, and (5) responsiveness.

What customers want reflects three levels of expectations—implicit expectations, explicit expectations, and latent expectations. Continuous improvement aims to delight customers by determining and meeting their latent expectations. Delighted customers are loyal customers. The customer criteria determined by researchers remain general and must be adapted to the expectations of specific customers.

ASSIGNMENT NOTES

1. This discussion is based on D. A. Garvin, "Competing on the Eight Dimensions of Quality," Harvard Business Review, November–December 1987, pp. 101-109.

2. This discussion is based on the findings of V.A. Zethaml, L.L. Berry, and P. Parasuraman, Delivering Quality Service: Balancing Customer Perceptions and Expectations (New York: Free Press, 1990) as reported by Tenner and DeToro in Total Quality Management, IIA Edition (Boston: Addison-Wesley, 1994).

The Voice of the Customer

Educational Objectives

After learning the content of this assignment, you should be able to:

▷ Distinguish between reactive and proactive methods of listening to the voice of the customer:

- Explain the relationship between understanding customer expectations and "zero defections."

- Describe the differences among and the uses of (a) internal benchmarking, (b) competitive benchmarking, (c) functional benchmarking, and (d) generic benchmarking.

- Given a hypothetical situation, recommend reactive and proactive methods of listening to the voice of the consumer.

▷ Explain the benefits of a customer orientation for insurance organizations.

The Voice of the Customer

METHODS FOR LISTENING TO THE VOICE OF THE CUSTOMER

Organizations that pursue continuous improvement must establish methods of gathering and evaluating information from customers.

Two general categories of methods for listening to the voice of the customer are **reactive methods** and **proactive methods**.

Reactive methods include these:

- Striving for zero defections
- Dealing with complaints, defections, and recoveries

Proactive methods include these:

- Conducting specifically tailored surveys
- Conducting personal interviews
- Using a mystery shopper
- Benchmarking

Reactive and proactive methods can be combined.

Reactive methods

The reactive methods of listening to the voice of the customer happen only when the customer initiates the communication.

Proactive methods

The proactive methods of listening to the voice of the customer are those in which organizations solicit feedback on products and services from customers.

Reactive Methods

Reactive methods of listening to the voice of the customer are those in which the communication is initiated by the customer. Every time a customer contacts an organization to ask a question, make a purchase, seek advice, or lodge a complaint, it is an opportunity for the organization to listen to and learn from the voice of the customer. Too often this potential source of valuable information is ignored. The customers' requests are handled in a routine way but without the information generated by these transactions being preserved, evaluated, or even drawn to the attention of the people in the organization who could make the best use of it.

Ignoring what might be learned from routine customer contacts simply represents a missed opportunity. No harm is done, but nothing is gained. Failing to learn from customer complaints, on the other hand, can do real harm. Complaints initiated by customers usually mean that those customers' implicit expectations are not being met, that what they thought could be taken for granted can no longer be. A customer who initiates a complaint frequently stands for numerous other customers who do not complain but rather silently take their business elsewhere. How customers' complaints are handled can determine whether those customers will stay loyal to the organization or take their business elsewhere, joining the ranks of "defecting customers." As continuous improvement students Frederick F. Reichheld and W. Earl Sasser, Jr., pointed out, "Defecting customers send a clear signal: profit slump ahead." Hearing that clear signal can be the result of a failure to listen to the voice of the customer.

Zero Defections

Philip B. Crosby, one of the best-known students of quality in manufacturing, launched a program called "Zero Defects" when he worked on the Pershing missile project at the Martin Marietta Corporation. One of Crosby's "Four Absolutes of Quality"[1] is to aim for zero defects as a realistic performance standard. See the exhibit "Crosby's Four Absolutes of Quality."

The costs of inspection, scrapping defective products, and redesigning and reworking defective products could exceed the investment to design a process that would yield outputs with zero defects. In other words, Crosby showed that the investment in quality could be profitable at a time when others still thought of it as a potentially beneficial expense.

Zero defections

A goal of organizations that aim to retain customers.

Reichheld and Sasser in a *Harvard Business Review* article took a similar approach by arguing that service organizations should aim for **zero defections** by "striving to keep every customer the company can profitably serve" and "mobilizing the organization to achieve" that aim. Here again, the attempt was to show that the investment in quality service could be profitable. The costs of losing customers could exceed the investment required to keep customers from defecting.

Several attempts have been made to quantify the improved profitability brought about by a decrease in customer defections. In some businesses, such calculations are easier to make than in others. The owner of some Domino's Pizza stores calculated that a regular customer was worth more than $5,000 over the life of a ten-year franchise contract. That demonstration was enough to motivate employees to strive for zero defections.

One study showed that if an insurance broker reduces customer defections by 5 percent, it would increase profits by 50 percent. This startling figure is based on a comparison of the net present values of profit streams from the average customer life at current defection rates, with the net present values of the profit streams for the average customer life at 5 percent lower defection rates.[2]

In the insurance business, preventing customer defections is most commonly discussed in terms of policyholder retention. Terri Daughters, of Nationwide Insurance Company, describes the costs to insurers of customer defections this way:

Crosby's Four Absolutes of Quality

1. Crosby's First Absolute of Quality is that the definition of quality is conformance to requirements, not goodness.

   Homeowners insurance consumers require sufficient insurance to cover their homes and contents in the event of any potential loss. They also require a reasonable rate for that insurance protection. They do not require payment for more coverage than the value of their homes and contents, since they can only expect to be reimbursed up to that value. "Goodness" might suggest the more coverage the better. It is for this reason that Crosby defines quality as *conformance to requirements* rather than "goodness."

2. Crosby's Second Absolute of Quality is that the system for causing quality is prevention, not appraisal.

   The 1-10-100 rule says the cost of a quality problem largely depends on when the problem is identified and resolved. The least costly problems ($1) are those that are prevented from happening and are caught and fixed in the work area. The problems and errors identified through inspection ($10) are still fixed internally but are caught and fixed after they have left the work area. The most costly problems and errors ($100) in terms of time and money are caught by the external customer. If a customer billing error is caught before the billing is actually mailed, the cost to correct the error is much less than if that inaccurate billing had actually been sent to a policyholder. Not only would additional administrative costs be incurred to correct the error but the customer would become involved, increasing the likelihood of dissatisfaction. The billing error would constitute a failed "moment of truth" for the organization.

3. Crosby's Third Absolute of Quality is that the performance standard for quality is zero defects, not "that's close enough." This absolute calls for a refusal to accept errors and to attack tenaciously the causes of errors until they are eliminated.

4. Crosby's Fourth Absolute of Quality is that the measurement of quality is the cost of nonconformance, not indexes. Counting the number of customer phone calls does not tell the principal of an insurance agency whether quality is improving. Computing the cost associated with clients who take their business elsewhere provides a more accurate measure of the cost of quality.

[DA04430]

The costs for losing . . . policyholders because of poor quality can be measured directly by the lost premium dollars and indirectly by the impact on the corporate expense ratio. Additional expense is incurred by having to write new business to compensate for losing old business. Naturally, writing new business is more expensive than maintaining existing business due to the underwriting, administrative, and agent commission costs. Studies have also shown that first-year policyholders generally do not have as good a loss ratio as longer-term policyholders, and loss costs directly impact a company's bottom line. The impact that is difficult to quantify is lost premiums of future policyholders. Some studies show that a happy customer tells three others, but an unhappy customer tells eleven other people.[3]

These direct and indirect costs clearly show the value of handling customer complaints well and learning from them.

Complaints, Defections, and Recoveries

Customers have implicit, explicit, and latent expectations about how complaints will be handled. Their experience as a result of lodging a complaint can be decisive for their long-term relationship with an organization. One of three results is likely to occur: (1) the way the complaint is handled will fail to meet their explicit expectations, their dissatisfaction will be increased, and they will become defectors; (2) the way the complaint is handled will meet their explicit expectations, their dissatisfaction will be minimized or neutralized, and they will view the organization in much the same way as they did before making the complaint; or (3) their explicit expectations will be exceeded, they will experience delight with the way the complaint is handled, and they will become more loyal than they had been before the complaint—they will be considered "**recoveries**."

Recoveries

Organizations achieve these when they handle complaints in such a way as to exceed customer expectations and gain customer loyalty.

Organizations that wish to gain recoveries rather than defectors frequently respond to complaints by overcompensating for the cause of the complaint and learning from customer complaints. This has led to the development of proactive ways of listening to the customer.

Proactive Methods

Based on the realization that customers' complaints provide valuable information, the most basic proactive methods of listening to the voice of the customer include soliciting and directing customer complaints, making it easy for customers to lodge them. An 800 telephone number dedicated to use by customers who have problems, concerns, or complaints represents such a proactive method. Employees who answer these phone calls are specifically trained to try to make recoveries of the callers and also to collect data on the callers and the nature of their complaints.

This data is then evaluated in an attempt to eliminate the causes of complaint and to improve the corresponding process, output, or outcome performance measures. In many ways, such 800 numbers are simply electronic versions of the old complaint or help desks long ago established in department and other retail stores. Many organizations now use Web sites to solicit feedback on products and services from customers. In all of these cases, the aim is to handle customer complaints in such a way that dissatisfied customers will become satisfied customers while the organization collects information that can help determine customers' implicit, explicit, and latent expectations.

Handling unsolicited complaints from customers, the reactive method of listening to the voice of the customer, is extremely limited with regard to understanding customer expectations for many reasons. First, those customers who lodge complaints represent a small and biased sample of the customer population. Second, customers frequently lodge complaints with a specific solution to their problem in mind. Third, customers who lodge complaints often reach someone who can solve their immediate problem but not implement permanent and widespread change. Fourth, because of the stressful circumstances of the transaction, the process is intended to solve an immediate problem, not increase an organization's understanding of its customers' expectations.

Many of these shortcomings are also true of hotlines, help desks, complaints solicited by Web sites, and so on. The most basic proactive methods of listening to the voice of the customer also reach a small and biased customer base and are also primarily designed to solve immediate problems. Increasing understanding of customer expectations is, at best, a secondary function.

Proactive methods of listening to the voice of the customer move from the most basic to the most sophisticated and from the least useful to the most useful as they become more and more specifically designed to solicit and evaluate information intended to illuminate customer expectations. Analyzing sales data, debriefing sales representatives, and conducting generalized customer service surveys are additional methods of soliciting information from or about customers. Some methods primarily or exclusively focus on customer expectations. These methods are frequently intended for use with a specific target market niche.

A market can be defined as a collection of customers or potential customers—a group of people or organizations with an identifiable need for a product or service. Every individual and organization in this country at this time could be said to make up the U.S. market for insurance because all of these individuals and organizations face the possibility of accidental financial losses.

Despite this common trait, it would be very difficult, if not impossible, for any single product or service to meet the extremely diverse needs of this market. For this reason, the large, diverse market is subdivided into market niches—smaller groups that have many more characteristics in common. People who drive cars make up a niche of the insurance market. Small business owners make up another niche. The farmers in a single state make up yet a third market niche. Insurance market niches can be determined in many ways—by the exposures to loss the customers face, by the potential size of the losses they face, by line of business, by territory, by premium volume, and so on.

A market niche becomes a **target market niche** when an organization decides to try to meet the needs of the customers in that niche. The way the insurance business is organized is related to target market niches. Insurance organizations might provide life and health insurance, property and liability insurance, or both. Insurance organizations might provide commercial insurance, personal insurance, or both. Some insurance organizations specialize in relatively small, narrow market niches—the professional liability exposures faced by healthcare providers, for example. No matter what the organization's target market niches are, the intention is to develop expertise in the insurance needs of the customers that make up those niches and meet those needs in a way that achieves customer satisfaction. Proactive methods of listening to the voice of the customer are designed to assist in the development of that expertise.

Target market niche

A collection of customers with similar characteristics that an organization identifies in order to meet their needs.

Specifically Tailored Surveys

Customers have become resistant to taking part in surveys. Part of the reason is that surveys are often general, lengthy, and lead to no follow-up. Surveys specifically tailored to a target market niche that are not too difficult or time consuming to complete can help organizations gain an understanding of customer expectations. Specifically tailored surveys are made for prospective customers and preexisting customers. See the exhibit "Prospective Customer Survey."

Personal Interviews

Personal interviews with customers, whether held on their own or to follow up on a survey, can also help organizations gain a fuller understanding of customer expectations. The key to conducting such interviews effectively is to use a few specific questions to urge the customer to talk and then listen. Skilled listening includes the ability to notice and interpret the choices of words or signs of passion displayed by the customers. If an interview becomes an attempt on the part of the organization to "educate" the customer or make a sales pitch, little knowledge of customer expectations will be gained and a satisfied, even loyal, customer could become dissatisfied. But if performed skillfully, interviews can provide a sense of even latent customer expectations.

Focus Groups

Focus group

A small group of customers or potential customers brought together to provide opinions about a specific product, service, need, or other issue.

A **focus group** is simply a meeting of a group of customers or prospective customers. They are frequently more effective than interviews with individual customers because attendees begin to talk to each other, comparing experiences and insights, so that the conversation becomes franker and less influenced by the presence of the organization's representatives. Focus groups are often good ways to follow up on survey results that need clarification. On the other hand, focus groups can also help organizations to learn the right questions to ask on future surveys.

Mystery Shopper

Mystery shopper

An employee or someone connected with an organization who pretends to be a customer to sample the organization's customer service.

The use of a **mystery shopper** is a way for an organization "to see itself as others see it," to paraphrase the Scottish poet Robert Burns. An employee or someone connected with the organization pretends to be a customer in order to sample the treatment customers receive. One of the principals of a large Midwestern insurance agency routinely has a friend or relative call his office and express an interest in changing insurance agencies. The principal then receives a report on what the caller experiences during and after the call. The senior managers of many organizations now periodically listen to customer phone conversations, monitoring the level of service provided, while learning about customer concerns, complaints, and expectations, a variation on the mystery shopper technique.

Prospective Customer Survey

New Customer Survey

1. Have you switched agents in the past 3 years?
   ❏ Yes   ❏ No

2. What type of agency do you currently use?
   ❏ An agent representing several insurance companies
   ❏ An agent representing only one company

3. On a scale of **1 (the lowest importance to you)** to **5 (the highest)**, how do you rate your expectations from your insurance agent:

Good coverage and value...1   2   3   4   5
- Finds the best coverage for you
- Understands your needs
- Gets you a good value for your money

Speed and accuracy...1   2   3   4   5
- Makes sure your bills are error free and policies are accurate
- Is available when you call
- Handles claims quickly

Knowledge 1   2   3   4   5
- Knowledgeable about different insurance products in general
- Knowledgeable specifically about the company's/companies' products
- Explains coverage

Professionalism...1   2   3   4   5
- Is very professional (e.g., excellent reputation in community; well-trained, knowledgeable staff)
- Offers discounts for multiple policies

Personal attention...1   2   3   4   5
- Takes time to talk to you personally
- Is friendly and caring

Quick service availability 1   2   3   4   5
- Quick service (e.g., prompt return of phone calls)
- More than one person in office available to help

Consulting 1   2   3   4   5
- Watches for products suited to you
- Keeps up with your needs
- Reviews policy at renewal
- Gives advice on protecting property

Represents a company you have heard of......................1   2   3   4   5

Gives you a choice of insurance companies,
and shops for the best price 1   2   3   4   5

Is available evenings and weekends 1   2   3   4   5
- By phone
- Office is open

Trustworthiness/stability...1   2   3   4   5
- Insures family member or friend
- How long in business

Is a personal friend 1   2   3   4   5

Adapted with permission from Quality Customer Service: An Idea Book for Your Independent Agency of the IIAA, Alexandria, VA. [DA04431]

Existing Customer Survey

Please complete the following using a scale of 1 to 5 with 1 the worst and 5 the best.

Customer service

		1	2	3	4	5
1.	Our staff provides courteous service	1	2	3	4	5
2.	Our customer service staff is knowledgeable	1	2	3	4	5
3.	Our staff is available when you call or visit	1	2	3	4	5
4.	We return your phone calls promptly	1	2	3	4	5
5.	We handle your claims fairly and promptly	1	2	3	4	5
6.	Management is available if problems arise	1	2	3	4	5
7.	Your agent tries to provide the best products for the best value	1	2	3	4	5
8.	Your agent gives accurate quotes	1	2	3	4	5
9.	Our staff keeps you updated on changes that may affect your coverage premium	1	2	3	4	5
10.	We take a consultative approach and recommend coverages when needed	1	2	3	4	5

General office operations

		1	2	3	4	5
1.	Our telephone system	1	2	3	4	5
2.	The automation/computer system we use	1	2	3	4	5
3.	Our office location	1	2	3	4	5
4.	Our office hours	1	2	3	4	5

Quality of products and companies represented

		1	2	3	4	5
1.	The insurance companies that we represent	1	2	3	4	5
2.	The competitiveness of our products	1	2	3	4	5
3.	The type of products that we offer	1	2	3	4	5

Overall rating of our agency

1. Why do you do business with our agency?

_____

_____

_____

2. What irritates you the most about doing business with us?

_____

_____

_____

3. If we could change just one thing or make just one aspect of your experience with us better, what would that be?

_____

_____

_____

Optional

Name: _____

Address: _____

_____

Phone: _____

Fax: _____

Adapted with permission from Quality Customer Service: An Idea Book for Your Independent Agency of the IIAA, Alexandria, VA. [DA04432]

Benchmarking

Benchmarking is basically an attempt to look at the world through the eyes of customers by engaging in comparative shopping. The practice requires that an organization or a department of an organization compare its own practices, procedures, processes, and products with those of others that are considered the best. Benchmarking can be internal, competitive, functional, or generic.

Internal benchmarking consists of comparing one department's procedures, processes, or products with those of other departments within the same organization. The information needed to make such comparisons is usually readily available, and this type of benchmarking is often convenient and relatively easy to carry out. An insurance company's customer service department might have spent a good deal of effort to train customer service representatives in telephone technique, for instance. Comparing the phone technique of customer service representatives with that of underwriters, for instance, could lead to changes that would improve the phone technique of underwriters. In this case, benchmarking found the department with the best phone technique within the organization and established the procedures and training used by that department as a standard for other departments to emulate and achieve.

Although internal benchmarking is the most convenient form of benchmarking, it is also the most limited. A more useful form of benchmarking is for one organization to compare its procedures, processes, and products with those of direct competitors, that is, to engage in competitive benchmarking. The insurance company that establishes its customer service department's phone technique as an internal benchmark, a company-wide standard, could also periodically compare the group's procedures and practices with those of other insurers who serve similar customers. **Competitive benchmarking** in this case could uncover ways to improve the phone technique of the customer service representatives, raising the standard to maintain a level of service comparable to that of competitors.

The insurance business has often been accused of being too inward looking. Because of the peculiar nature of the insurance product, it has considered itself so different from other businesses that it could not learn from them. Functional benchmarking is a way to overcome this criticism. **Functional benchmarking** requires that an organization compare how it performs a function with the ways same or at least similar functions are performed by organizations from other businesses or industries. An insurance company should not be satisfied with the phone practices of its customer service representatives simply because it meets or even exceeds the standards of competitors. Instead, the organization should compare its practices with those of customer service groups in other industries. A Common Reader, a mail-order bookseller, provides high-quality service through effective use of the telephone. The insurance company might certainly learn about phone technique by comparing its own practices with those of a recognized quality leader, even though that quality leader happens to be in the retail book business.

Internal benchmarking
Comparing one department's procedures, processes, or products with those of other departments within the same organization.

Competitive benchmarking
Comparing one organization's procedures, processes, and products with those of a direct competitor.

Functional benchmarking
Compares how organizations from dissimilar businesses perform similar functions.

Generic benchmarking

A search for the best approach and can lead to new ways of performing functions.

Distinguishing functional benchmarking from **generic benchmarking** can be difficult. They differ in that the comparisons required for generic benchmarking are not limited to internal departments of an organization, competitors, or even similar functions performed in other industries, but rather they represent the search for "the best of the best" in that they can reveal totally new approaches or methods. For instance, the insurance company that compares its phone technique with that of A Common Reader could be led to examine how other mail-order booksellers operate. Such an examination could lead the insurer to consider performing its customer service function in a completely different way, without the phone at all, perhaps through a Web site, for instance, modeled on that of Amazon.com or some other virtual bookseller.

If internal benchmarking is the most convenient but also the most limited type of benchmarking, generic benchmarking is the most difficult type but also potentially the most rewarding. It should be clear that the use of benchmarking as a search for the best of the best epitomizes continuous improvement.

Reactive and Proactive Methods Combined

The primary reason for listening to the voice of the customer is to obtain the fullest understanding possible of customer expectations. To that end, organizations use a combination of reactive and proactive methods. It is clear that many of these methods overlap or can best be used in combination. The most effective combination of methods for any given organization at any given time cannot be determined in advance. Listening to the voice of the customer is itself a continuous process that is constantly subject to improvement.

All the same, an idea of the power of using various methods in combination can be estimated through reference to a customer orientation continuum cube, which displays the relationships among the levels of performance measures, the levels of customer expectations, and both reactive and proactive methods of listening to the customer. In this respect, it does much to summarize what is meant by customer orientation. See the exhibit "Customer Orientation Continuum Cube."

Customer orientation is at its lowest when an organization is unaware of its customers' implicit expectations, the expectations customers take for granted. Unsolicited complaints, the reactive method of listening to the voice of the customer, are a sign that an organization no longer meets its customers' implicit expectations. Customer orientation is at its highest when an organization is aware of its customers' latent expectations, the expectations customers themselves are unaware of or are unable to articulate. The model in the customer orientation continuum cube shows that an organization with dissatisfied customers is in a position to delight customers. What might be misleading about this model is that it appears static. The situation it depicts, however, is far from static. Customers who were once delighted because their latent expectations were met can become dissatisfied customers because their

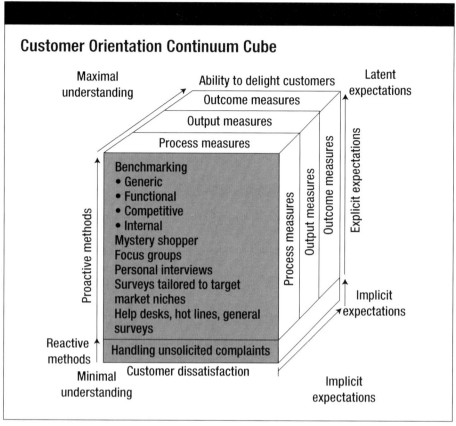

Customer Orientation Continuum Cube

[DA04433]

implicit expectations are no longer met. Customer orientation requires fluidity and flexibility in order for organizations to understand and meet or exceed the changing expectations of customers.

THE BENEFITS OF CUSTOMER ORIENTATION

Insurance companies should concentrate on customer orientation.

The advantages of a customer orientation for insurance organizations—the ability to define customer expectations in order to improve processes continuously, increased policyholder retention, and enhanced new product development—should provide a focus to process improvement efforts.

A news story in an insurance trade magazine announced changes in the structure of a property and liability insurance company that distributes its products through brokers and independent agents. The gist of the story was that the insurer had "grouped its businesses according to how it sells products with hopes that the company can improve distribution to brokers and agents." The insurer formed three business units: the Business Customer Group, the Individual and Family Customer Group, and the International Customer

Group. "The new distribution platform will give agents and brokers easier access to our products," a spokesperson for the company said.

This news story shows an insurance company striving to become customer oriented. Its new structure is clearly not defined by a product line or distribution method but rather by the nature of the end users each business unit is designed to serve—businesses, individuals and families, and international clients. The names of the units imply a customer orientation; they are defined by target market niches. Despite that, the description of the reasons for the new structure concentrates on products and distribution without ever referring to customers for at least two reasons. First, the company's top management is accustomed to thinking in terms of products and distribution but not in terms of customers. Second, a company that does not sell and service its products directly to end users must view its distribution system as its primary external customers, and doing so necessarily complicates all references to and discussion of customers.

Despite these limitations, the Business Customer Group is designed to communicate clearly not only to brokers and agents but also to businesses with insurance needs in a way that the Commercial Property Underwriting Unit, for instance, never did. The new system groups traditionally separate and distinct functions—marketing, underwriting, and claims—and that shows a real attempt to become customer oriented.

What are the benefits of such a cross-functional system? The most obvious answer is that the insurer is now organized in a way that should lead to a fuller understanding of customer expectations. As a result of that fuller understanding, the insurer should be in a better position to attract and retain customers through the ability to meet if not exceed their expectations, that is, through the ability to provide quality products and services. Policyholder retention, the attempt to strive for zero defections, is one concrete benefit of customer orientation that should improve profitability. But it is not the only one. Two other benefits are new product development and process improvement.

Policyholder Retention

Insurance organizations with a customer orientation use proactive methods of listening to the voice of the customer that are designed specifically to support their policyholder retention efforts. Because agents, brokers, and companies have a common interest in this subject, they often work together on it. Those companies that distribute their products through agents and brokers can only retain policyholders through the efforts of the agents and brokers with whom they work. The results of surveys conducted by some such companies in conjunction with the Independent Insurance Agents Association can be displayed in chart form. See the exhibit "Personal Lines and Commercial Lines Policyholder Retention."

The surveys used were clearly specific—that is, more proactive than general surveys. The surveys were specific in two ways: first, they sought to determine

Personal Lines and Commercial Lines Policyholder Retention

Personal Lines Policyholder Retention
Retention Depends on Professionalism, Value, Accuracy, and Helpfulness

Commercial Lines Policyholder Retention
Retention Depends on Quick Service, Value, and Understanding the Company's Needs

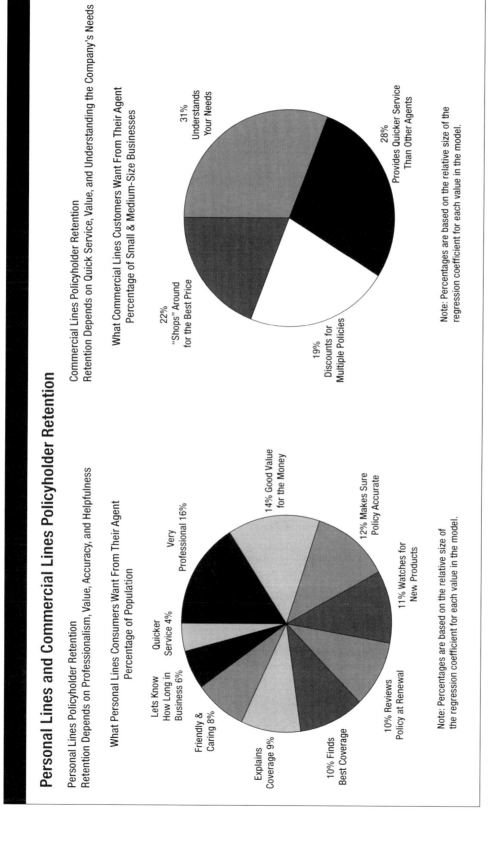

What Personal Lines Consumers Want From Their Agent
Percentage of Population

- Very Professional 16%
- Quicker Service 4%
- Lets Know How Long in Business 6%
- Friendly & Caring 8%
- Explains Coverage 9%
- 10% Finds Best Coverage
- 10% Reviews Policy at Renewal
- 11% Watches for New Products
- 12% Makes Sure Policy Accurate
- 14% Good Value for the Money

Note: Percentages are based on the relative size of the regression coefficient for each value in the model.

What Commercial Lines Customers Want From Their Agent
Percentage of Small & Medium-Size Businesses

- 31% Understands Your Needs
- 28% Provides Quicker Service Than Other Agents
- 22% "Shops" Around for the Best Price
- 19% Discounts for Multiple Policies

Note: Percentages are based on the relative size of the regression coefficient for each value in the model.

Adapted with permission from Quality Customer Service: An Idea Book for Your Independent Agency of the IIAA, Alexandria, VA. [DA04434]

what consumers want from agents in terms that are relevant for policyholder retention; second, the surveys were specifically designed for use with two different target market niches, personal lines consumers and commercial lines customers that operate small or medium-sized businesses.

The survey results in both cases can be seen as a refinement of or an elaboration on "faster, better, cheaper." Price and speed or convenience of service are clearly of interest to both sets of customers. As might be expected, they are of greater interest to commercial lines customers than to personal lines consumers. But both sets of customers show a strong interest in "better" and indicate what that means to them. In both cases, the responses with the highest percentages—"very professional" for personal lines customers and "understands your needs" for commercial lines customers—are related to quality. Agents, brokers, and companies that solicit and interpret this kind of information from their customers are in a position to act on it and thus improve policyholder retention.

New Product Development

New product development

Consists of identifying unmet customer expectations or needs and developing products to meet those needs.

A customer orientation assists insurance organizations in **new product development** because customers are the biggest single source of new product ideas. Most new products, of course, are not totally new in the sense that nothing like them previously existed. Instead, they represent modifications of or enhancements to existing products. Listening to the voice of the customer is a way to become aware of potentially successful modifications to existing products. Perhaps the most successful new products are developed as a result of the identification of an unmet latent customer expectation.

It is now difficult to imagine personal lines insurance without the homeowners policy. Nevertheless, it was once a new product, a modification to existing products designed to meet an unmet need of consumers. H. R. Heilman described the situation that led to the introduction of the homeowners policy this way:

> A survey made in 1949 showed that many families had never been solicited for insurance beyond that which their mortgagee required. Fire insurance was usually written for the amount of the mortgage and was not increased to follow the inflationary upsweep of values. Personal property was even less adequately covered, and relatively few individuals bought personal liability or theft insurance. These essential coverages were not bought because the insurance agent could not afford to sell them. The small premium that each separate contract would develop was inadequate to justify the expense of soliciting, policywriting, and premium collecting. The obvious need was for a simple package policy combining all these coverages with a convenient installment payment plan.
>
> In the fall of 1950 the Insurance Company of North America introduced the first Homeowners Policies which did all these things. One of these contracts, the Homeowners Comprehensive Policy, contained all the distinctive features which today set Homeowners Policies and rating plans apart from other kinds of insurance.[4]

What Heilman clarifies elsewhere is that this "obvious need" went unmet for a long time because insurance regulation then prevented the development and sale of "multi-lines" policies—that is, insurance companies were then licensed to sell only property insurance or only casualty (liability) insurance, not both. Meeting the needs of the growing numbers of homeowners meant not only identifying that customer need but also bringing about regulatory change. John Diemand, then the president of the Insurance Company of North America, is generally credited with pioneering the homeowners policy by identifying the customer need and working for regulatory change that would allow his company and others to meet that need. He seems to have had in mind as a model the householders comprehensive policy that had been developed in England and sold by Lloyd's as early as 1914.

Diemand chaired a committee of the National Association of Insurance Commissioners (NAIC) that bore his name, the Diemand Committee, which investigated and made recommendations on the possibilities for multiple lines insurance in the United States in 1943. Multiple lines legislation passed in Pennsylvania in 1949, the same year the consumer survey discussed above by Heilman was conducted. The legislation reflected the recommendations of the Diemand Committee.

Why did John Diemand see the applicability and profitability of a version of an English insurance policy in the United States early and urge legislative change that would permit its introduction? He attributed it to what would now be called a closeness to the customer, a knowledge of a potential target market niche. "In my own territory," he said, "I am thinking of the 400,000 individually owned homes in Philadelphia. . . .I think that form can be made to appeal to that particular [market]." By 1951, a multiple lines rating bureau was organized. In 1953, homeowners premiums reached $2,900,000.

John Diemand's familiarity with his company's territory, with the row houses of Philadelphia and the insurance needs of the families who lived in them, brought about not only a new product that is now taken for granted but also a dramatic change in the regulation and structure of the insurance business. A closeness to the customer continues to be the basis of new insurance products—from loss control services provided on a fee basis to employment practices liability coverage.

An opportunity exists when a market— a collection of potential customers with similar characteristics—expresses an unmet need. Opportunities are most likely to be identified by those organizations that maintain contact with customers and gather information from them. In short, listening to the voice of the customer gives organizations the information they need to develop new products successfully.

Process Improvement

The most important benefit of a customer orientation for insurance organizations is the ability to define customer expectations in order to improve processes continuously. Process improvement is the second key element of continuous improvement because an organization's processes determine what customers receive and how they receive it. The gap between what the process produces (the voice of the process) and what customers expect (the voice of the customer) points in a measurable way to which processes are in the greatest need of improvement and in what way, and establishes standards by which to determine when improvement has in fact taken place.

Today there exists an emphasis on insurance products, which tend to be relatively uniform, rather than on the delivery of the promise at the center of all insurance products. The delivery, the fulfillment of that promise, always necessarily varies.

SUMMARY

Reactive methods of listening to the voice of the customer are based on those communications that are initiated by customers. Unsolicited complaints from customers are an example of a reactive method. The purpose of making the most of these contacts is to retain customers, to strive for what Reichheld and Sasser called "zero defections." The direct and indirect costs of losing customers clearly demonstrate the advantage of handling customer complaints well.

Proactive methods expand on this idea. Organizations use these methods to initiate communications with customers. Phone lines with 800 numbers that are dedicated to helping customers with complaints or concerns represent a basic proactive method of communicating with customers. The most basic proactive methods tend to serve a couple of purposes at once. More sophisticated proactive methods are designed specifically to gather and analyze information on customer expectations.

Customers are often organized into target market niches for analysis. A target market niche is a collection of customers with similar needs that an organization determines to try to meet. Surveys, interviews, focus groups, mystery shoppers, and benchmarking are some frequently used proactive methods for listening to the voice of the customer. Organizations that try to hear and understand the full range of the customer's voice combine the use of both reactive and proactive methods.

Some of the advantages for insurance organizations that listen to the voice of the customer are increased policyholder retention, enhanced new product development, and a focus that will provide guidance for process improvement efforts.

ASSIGNMENT NOTES

1. Philip B. Crosby, Quality Is Free: The Art of Making Quality Certain (New York: Mentor Books, 1979).
2. F.E. Reichheld and W. E. Sasser, Jr., "Zero Defections: Quality Comes to Services," Harvard Business Review, September-October 1990, pp. 105-111.
3. Terri Daughters, "Quality and the Bottom Line."
4. H. R. Heilman, "Homeowners and Other Personal Packages," in John D. Long and Davis W. Gregg, Property and Liability Insurance Handbook (Homewood, Ill.: Richard D. Irwin, 1965), pp. 747-757.

Direct Your Learning ▶▶

5

Key Processes

After learning the content of this assignment, you should be able to:

▶ Describe key processes.

▶ Describe a work process model.

▶ Summarize the questions that need to be asked to identify key processes.

▶ Given a case, describe the elements of process management and summarize key processes.

▶▶

Key Processes

IDENTIFYING KEY PROCESSES

Just as customer orientation begins with identification of customers, process improvement begins with identification of key processes.

What are an organization's key processes, how can they be identified, and what does process management mean? Like customer identification, process identification is not a simple matter. Instead, process identification can prompt a thoughtful analysis of a department, an organization, or a business.

Finding the Essence

Bill O'Brien, one of the pioneers of continuous improvement in the insurance business and a former president and chief executive officer (CEO) of The Hanover Insurance Company, wrote this:

> At Hanover, we asked ourselves: "What's the essence of a property and liability insurance company?" Ultimately, we said it was twofold. In part, insurance depends on the management of probabilities: Would you write a particular insurance deal at 20 cents? How about at 12 cents? In that sense, insurance businesses are like networks of bookie joints, betting on high school basketball games.
>
> But the business also depends upon quality relationships with customers. I have seen insurance companies throw away fortunes by moving into the wholesale use of the telephone to settle claims. This worked all right for small claims, like a broken windshield. But insurance managers who understood the importance of relationships knew when to stop. They knew that a mere telephone response to a bad bodily injury would send claimants running to trial lawyers.
>
> Companies that tried extensive telephone settlement found out the hard way: At first, it was beautiful. They got rid of many high-salaried claims adjusters. But those savings, and then some, got eaten up in litigation costs, lost customers, and expensive settlements.[1]

What Bill O'Brien is doing in this statement is talking about work or, more specifically, identifying key processes. The statement deserves to be considered in some detail.

How does he proceed? By asking one fundamental question, answering it, and refining the answers with analogies and examples drawn from experience.

The fundamental question is: "What's the essence of a property and liability insurance company?" "Essence" is, in some respects, an odd word in this context. It has a long philosophical tradition and carries the sense of intangibility. But the statement goes on to clarify that it is used here to mean what is essential. This sense becomes clear from the use of the phrase "depends on" in the two answers to the question. O'Brien and others at Hanover asked themselves, in other words, "What must a property and liability insurance company do?" In the language of continuous improvement, this question would read: "What are a property and liability insurance company's key processes?"

Advocates of continuous improvement consider work to be a process, a sequence of steps that results in a product or a service, an output. What a property and liability insurance company does can be described in terms of an extremely large number of processes. What a property and liability insurance company must do, what activities are essential to it, can be described in terms of a relatively small number of **key processes**.

Key process

A work process that is essential to an organization and that has the greatest influence on customers.

Insurance Key Processes

O'Brien's answer limits these key processes to two. His answer begins, "In part, insurance depends on the management of probabilities." It concludes, ". . . the business also depends upon quality relationships with customers." For O'Brien, in other words, these are a property and liability insurance company's two key processes:

• Managing probabilities
• Establishing and managing quality relationships with customers

Both of these processes are described in general, abstract, and even vague terms. Neither "managing probabilities" nor "managing quality relationships" draws pictures of people in action doing specific things. No doubt for this reason O'Brien quickly provides very specific examples: "Would you write a particular insurance deal for 20 cents? How about at 12 cents? In that sense, insurance businesses are like networks of bookie joints, betting on high school basketball games."

Another insurance person might have said that one of an insurance company's key processes is underwriting—deciding whether to write a piece of business and, if so, under what conditions and at what price. Similarly, he provides a concrete example of managing quality relationships with customers or, rather, how some companies failed to manage them: "I have seen insurance companies throw away fortunes by moving into the wholesale use of the telephone to settle claims." Another insurance person might have said that another key process for an insurance company is handling claims—determining whether a loss is covered and, if so, how it should be settled.

This suggests that Bill O'Brien's statement could be reduced to: "What are a property and liability insurance company's key processes? Underwriting and claim handling." Reducing O'Brien's statement to this simple answer might seem helpful. If he is right, every insurance company would know for all time what its key processes are and would never have to consider the question again. That might seem helpful but it in fact would be disastrous. O'Brien's statement cannot be reduced in this way because what is lost in such a translation is thought. The most important word in his statement is "ultimately"—"What's the essence of a property and liability insurance company? Ultimately, we said it was twofold."

No doubt much time, energy, and effort were spent between the raising of the question and the formulation of the answer—an answer that was not true for all companies, at all times, and under all circumstances, but for the executives in that time and place who devised and agreed on the answer. What is learned about a department, an organization, or a business by raising the question of what its key processes are and thinking through the answers is at least as valuable as the answers to the question themselves.

A WORK PROCESS MODEL

Just as customer orientation begins with the identification of customers, process improvement begins with the identification of processes and a determination as to which processes are key.

Before the identification of key processes is discussed, it will be helpful to consider work processes in more detail. Nonetheless, the fundamental definition of a work process—a sequence of steps that results in a product or service, an output—remains the same.

Four identifiable groups of people are involved with every work process:

1. The customer
2. The work group
3. The supplier
4. The owner

Work Process Groups

These roles are not fixed and permanent. Instead, the roles may shift often, almost constantly, but are always defined by a position in the work process.

Brief definitions of these groups will help show how they are related to a position in a process.

Customers are the people who receive the output, the product or service the work process is designed to produce. Customers might use the output on its own or as the input for another work process.

The **work group** consists of the people whose work produces the output. The **suppliers** are the people who provide inputs to the work process. (This means that the work group is the customer of the supplier.) The **owner** is the person or persons who are responsible for the output and for the operation and improvement of the process.

Work group

Consists of one or more workers who produce an output.

Supplier

A person who provides inputs to a work group.

Owner

The person responsible for the output and for the operation and improvement of the work process.

The Work Process Model

The work process begins and ends with the customer. Customers, through their requirements, define the attributes of the output. When customers receive and use the output, they provide feedback on it that might alter the requirements and redefine the desired attributes of the output.

QUESTIONS THAT IDENTIFY KEY PROCESSES

Any strategy for continuous improvement requires a way to identify key processes.

Bill O'Brien of The Hanover Insurance Company said, with regard to continuous improvement, that cooks came before cookbooks. The approach he took to key process identification at Hanover was homegrown and homemade; it arose naturally, out of his own temperament and out of the circumstances and people that then existed at the company.

There are clear advantages to working in this way. Different cooks, using the same recipe, notoriously do not come up with identical, interchangeable dishes. Nonetheless, students of continuous improvement have gathered and analyzed the practices of numerous organizations and have tried to deduce from those practices a systematic approach for identifying key processes.

Key processes can be identified by raising four questions:

1. Which outputs are of the greatest importance to customers?
2. Which processes produce these outputs?
3. Which processes are most visible to customers?
4. Of the processes identified in response to Questions 2 and 3, which seem to have the greatest potential for improvement?

The nature of these questions reflects a broad conception of what key processes are. Key processes are primarily those processes that have the greatest influence on customers. The final question goes a step further by identifying those key processes that might provide the greatest increase in customer satisfaction through improvement. The benefits of using this type of approach to key process identification are (1) it emphasizes customers and (2) it allows for the identification of **cross-functional processes**.

Cross-functional process

A work process performed by people in separate organizations, departments, and divisions.

Organizational structures are often the reflections of internal considerations; that is, they are not always customer-oriented. Processes that are the most crucial for customer satisfaction often cross organizational, departmental, or functional lines. In such cases, the processes are segmented by department or function and are frequently designed to meet goals or objectives without regard to the needs or expectations of customers.

The four questions for key process identification are designed to identify those processes with the greatest influence on customer satisfaction without regard to organizational structure, the relative influence of various department heads, office politics, and similar gunk. Just as drawing a model of a work process can reveal how things are actually done, identifying key processes can cause an organization to focus on those internal processes that are of greatest importance to its customers and enlist customers as co-producers.

Raising and answering these four questions for a property and liability insurance company clarify why Bill O'Brien's statement (that insurance depends on the management of probabilities and also depends upon quality relationships with customers) cannot be reduced to the identification of two key processes—underwriting and claim handling. Doing so is a fundamental error in thought, a confusion of categories, mistaking an example for an answer.

Customers might feel that receiving timely, accurate, and understandable bills is very important to them. Neither the underwriting process nor the claim-handling process will cause a company to meet that customer expectation. On the other hand, O'Brien's broad statement—". . . the business also depends upon quality relations with customers"—or the first three questions posed for key process identification would lead to a consideration of the billing expectations of the company's customers.

Process improvement is the second element of continuous improvement, following customer orientation, because processes cannot be evaluated, much less improved, without a thorough understanding of customer expectations.

PROCESS MANAGEMENT AND KEY PROCESSES

One result of the application of the ideas of continuous improvement is a shift in emphasis from employee performance problems to process problems.

A performance problem suggests that one or more processes are in need of improvement. This shift has led some students of continuous improvement to consider the elements of **process management**.[2]

Process Management

Basically, these are the five elements of process management:

1. Process ownership
2. Process planning
3. Process control
4. Process measurement
5. Process improvement

An example should help clarify the roles of both ownership and planning in process management. See the exhibit "The Underwriter Who Cried High Priority."

Process management

Involves the ownership, planning, control, measurement, and improvement of a work process.

Process ownership

Taking responsibility for a process's design, operation, and improvement.

Process planning

Documenting, defining, and understanding the parts and the interrelationship of the parts of each process.

Process control

Ensuring that outputs are predictable and consistent with customer expectations.

Process measurement

Mapping performance attributes of the process and establishing criteria for evaluating them.

Process improvement

This involves increasing the effectiveness of the process.

The Underwriter Who Cried High Priority

An Example of the Roles of Process Ownership and Planning

Concetta Altimara, a commercial accounts producer with Mid-City Insurance Agency had been calling on House and Haul, a warehousing and shipping operation, for some time with little success, unable to have a chance to even quote on the business. Recently, House and Haul decided to move into a newly constructed facility in a suburban industrial park. Frank Otter, House and Haul's treasurer, decided to obtain bids on the property insurance for the new building. He called Concetta and asked her to prepare a quote for him by June 1, then about a month away.

Concetta was elated that she would finally have a chance to quote on at least some of House and Haul's business. She alerted two underwriters she had worked with in the past, emphasizing her deadline, and asked for their help in competing for the business. Brad Tompkins, at Insure-All, did not sound particularly enthusiastic but agreed to work with Concetta on developing the quote. Charlene Jenkins, with IIA Insurance Company, said that new construction in the area to which House and Haul was moving was of real interest to her company and she was anxious to do all she could to help Concetta obtain the business.

Concetta set to work preparing submissions for both companies— completing applications for insurance, obtaining photographs of the property, attaching recent financial statements on House and Haul's operation, supplying literature on the industrial park, and providing brief biographies of the potential client's management team. In a cover letter to each underwriter, she stated again her deadline of June 1 and asked to be notified immediately if more information was needed. She followed up by phone to confirm that the submissions had been received and again offered to obtain additional information.

Brad Tompkins at Insure-All liked the look of Concetta's submission, requested a loss control inspection and recommendation on the facility, and started to underwrite the business as submitted.

Charlene Jenkins called the head of the Loss Control Department to request that Concetta's submission be given a high priority. She explained that it was the kind of business the company was anxious to write but that a fairly quick turnaround was required if it were to compete for the business. The head of Loss Control explained to Charlene that the department was short-handed. He also said underwriters thought every submission should be given a high priority. "If everything is given special treatment, nothing is," he said. "We work on a first come, first served basis. That's fair. Just send your request over, and we'll deal with it."

A week before the deadline, Brad Tompkins provided Concetta with a quote that was not very aggressively priced or creatively underwritten. Concetta had not yet heard from Charlene Jenkins and phoned her. Charlene explained that she was still waiting for a loss control report and recommendation. Everything else was complete, but she was not free to issue a quote without those documents. She told Concetta she had requested that the submission be given a high priority.

On June 1, Concetta presented a proposal to Frank Otter on House and Haul's property insurance based on Brad Tompkins's quotation. The business would be acceptable to Insure-All. Otter accepted the proposal two days later, saying that it was neither the lowest nor the highest bid he had received but he had been impressed by the thoroughness of Concetta's work and the promptness with which Insure-All's inspector had turned up at the new building.

[DA04444]

Process Ownership and Process Planning

As illustrated in the Mid-City Insurance Agency case, unclear ownership of a process can have disastrous results. In this case, the overall process—competing for new commercial lines property business—is not only cross-functional but involves more than one organization, Mid-City Insurance Agency, Insure-All, and IIA Insurance.

The underwriting process breaks down at the IIA Insurance Company through an apparent but unacknowledged conflict over the ownership of a process. The commercial lines underwriters are dependent on loss control inspectors but have no authority and little influence over them. Charlene Jenkins assumes that the way to expedite loss control inspections, reports, and recommendations is to request priority service from the head of the Loss Control Department.

The Loss Control Department head does not believe in priority service and has established a policy of performing inspections on a "first come, first served" basis. Charlene's apparent inability to do anything about this fundamental conflict again suggests, at best, unclear ownership of the process. She neither contacts a loss control specialist directly nor goes to her own department head with the problem. The situation is typical of chronic "turf battles" in organizations. No one is clearly designated the owner of the process—responsible for its design, operation, and improvement.

Similarly, it appears unlikely that anyone at IIA Insurance has done process planning, at least with regard to commercial lines underwriting. No one has seen to it that the parts and interrelationship of the parts of each process are documented, defined, and understood. On the contrary, because commercial lines underwriting and loss control are separate departments, their activities are viewed as separate, distinct, and unrelated processes. The result is what some commentators call "lack of alignment" in cross-functional processes and others, more accurately and refreshingly, call "craziness."

What emphasizes the craziness in this case is that IIA's marketing department and underwriting guidelines appear to have targeted the type of business Concetta submitted. From the standpoint of IIA's potential customers—Concetta Altimara and, ultimately, Frank Otter—the company behaves in a way that suggests it has no interest in writing the business at all. Craziness of this type—an almost complete lack of contact with reality—is not rare in the business world generally nor in the insurance business in particular. But it takes an effort to spot it, diagnose it, and do something about it.

Identifying and managing key processes are crucial for any organization that intends to diminish its crazy behavior and meet the needs of its customers. Some insurance companies have restructured or reorganized with this end in view, establishing teams of underwriters, marketing specialists, loss control people, and claim handlers that are trained and dedicated to serve target market niches. The restructuring is designed to avoid the problems caused by cross-functional processes. But assigning ownership of a process and engaging in process planning are not on their own sufficient. Process improvement, what some have called the heart of continuous improvement, is also necessary.

SUMMARY

Among the large set of processes carried out by an organization, those that are essential constitute a smaller set of key processes. One view holds that a property and liability insurance company's two key processes are (1) managing probabilities and (2) establishing and managing quality relationships with customers.

Four identifiable groups of people are involved with every work process:

1. The customer
2. The work group
3. The supplier
4. The owner

The work process model begins and ends with the customer.

The process improvement model is a set of six steps designed to be a guide to process improvement, not a rigid set of rules. These are the steps in the process improvement model:

1. Which outputs are of the greatest importance to customers?
2. Which processes produce these outputs?
3. Which processes are most visible to customers?
4. Of the processes identified in response to Questions 2 and 3, which seem to have the greatest potential for improvement?

Process management consists of five elements:

1. Process ownership
2. Process planning
3. Process control
4. Process measurement
5. Process improvement

The main reason for identifying key processes is to improve them.

ASSIGNMENT NOTES

1. Bill O'Brien, "What Do I Believe Is the Essence of My Business?" in Peter Senge, The Dance of Change (New York: Doubleday/Currency, 1999), pp. 236-237.
2. This discussion is adapted from "Six Ingredients of Process Management" in Arthur R. Tenner and Irving J. DeToro, Total Quality Management, IIA Edition (Reading, Mass.: Addison-Wesley, 1994), pp. 83-86.

Direct Your Learning ▶▶

6

The Process Improvement Model

Educational Objectives

After learning the content of this assignment, you should be able to:

▶ Describe the six steps in the process improvement model.

▶ Restate specific objectives in terms of the process.

▶ Distinguish between the voice of the customer and the voice of the process.

▶ Given a case, apply the process improvement model.

The Process Improvement Model | 6

THE SIX-STEP PROCESS IMPROVEMENT MODEL

The six steps in the process improvement model are generalizations that reflect the experiences of people who have actually attempted to improve a wide range of business processes. The result is a suggested guide to process improvement rather than a rigid set of infallible rules.[1]

Actually engaging in a process improvement model necessarily differs from reading a description of it. The advantage to becoming familiar with all six steps in the appropriate sequence is that it provides a check on thoroughness. Attempts at process improvement can be frustrated and lead to disappointment if one or more steps in this model are *unintentionally* skipped. When reviewing the steps in the process improvement model, apply the steps to a process or processes that you perform personally, such as processing new business submissions.

Almost inevitably, people who engage in process improvement find that they have to proceed through these six steps:

1. Defining the problem in terms of the process
2. Identifying and documenting the process
3. Measuring performance
4. Understanding why
5. Developing and testing ideas
6. Implementing solutions and evaluating them, including the documentation of results

Some people might describe these steps in different words or include more or fewer steps. They might assume the process has been identified and documented and eliminate Step 2, for instance. Others might argue that some of the steps are performed simultaneously. For example, understanding why necessarily leads to ideas for solutions to the problem, almost merging Steps 4 and 5. Still others could think that documenting results is so important it should be a seventh step.

Step 1—Defining the Problem in Terms of the Process

What kind of problems are addressed by process improvement? Process improvement can address an endless variety of problems, but they all have one thing in common—customer expectations are not being met. The problem can involve internal customers, external customers, or both. No matter what the nature of the problem is or the types of customers involved, defining the problem in terms of the process begins by answering these five questions:

1. What is the output?
2. Who are the customers?
3. What are the customers' requirements?
4. Which process or processes produce the output?
5. Who are the owners of the process or processes involved?

The inability to answer one or more of these questions in a specific way reveals immediate steps that need to be taken before process improvement can proceed. If ownership of the process has not been assigned, for instance, it should be. If the customers' requirements are unclear, they should be clarified through the use of the techniques described in earlier assignments.

On the other hand, the answers to these questions should provide the background for defining the problem in terms of the process. Consider the case of an insurance company employee who is unable to obtain a loss control report and recommendation in the time required by a customer. A traditional way of dealing with the problem is by attempting to resolve it as a discrete, one-time problem not seen in terms of a process. In other words, the insurer's employee could define the problem this way: "The loss control report for our potential client needs to be expedited." The insurer's employee could attempt to solve the problem by alerting the head of the loss control department to it and requesting priority service—a discrete, one-time solution to the problem that does not involve process improvement. A definition of the same problem in terms of the process might read: "The process of conducting loss control inspections and preparing reports and recommendations needs to be improved in order to meet customer expectations in terms of accuracy and timeliness." This definition of the problem would insist on very different possible solutions to it—solutions that would potentially remain invisible without this redefinition and restatement of the problem.

Step 2—Identifying and Documenting the Process

Flowchart

A diagram that graphically and sequentially depicts the activities of a particular organization or process.

Graphic depictions of work processes, whether or not accompanied by written or verbal descriptions, help clarify how work is actually accomplished. Identifying and documenting the process requires preparing such a graphic depiction—usually a **flowchart**. Preparing the flowchart often consists of making a picture of the answers to the questions raised in Step 1. Consider a simple flowchart that depicts IIA Insurance Company's loss control inspection request process. See the exhibit "Flowchart of IIA Insurance Company's Loss Control Inspection Request Process."

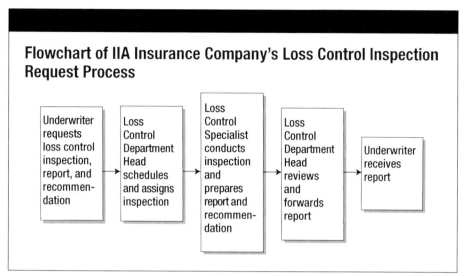

Flowchart of IIA Insurance Company's Loss Control Inspection Request Process

[DA04448]

A flowchart is simple in part because it takes a narrow view of the process. For example, the flowchart is not designed to consider the loss control inspection request process as a subset of larger processes—IIA's underwriting and marketing processes, for instance. The flowchart also is not designed to consider any external customers or the ultimate end user. The aim of the flowchart at this step is to clarify what currently takes place. This clarification should achieve four purposes:

- All of the participants in the process are identified by name, job title, or function and, if necessary, by department and organization.
- All of the participants in the process acquire a shared understanding of all of the steps in the process and of their own roles in it.
- All unnecessary steps, wasteful steps, bottlenecks, or causes of confusion in the process become visible.
- All likely ways of measuring process performance become identifiable.

Preparing flowcharts is never an end in itself. Flowcharts are valuable only as working documents, convenient ways for the participants in a process to become more aware of the process, their roles in it, and how it produces the outputs that it does.

Step 3—Measuring Performance

The concept of measuring on three levels can be clarified and expanded: the three levels of measurement are the process level, the output level, and the outcome level.

Process measures establish performance standards for the activities and operations that make up the process itself.

Output measures establish criteria, specific characteristics or attributes, of the output from two perspectives—the requirements of the customer and the capability of the process. The requirements of the customer, also known as the voice of the customer, define the quality of the output the process *should* produce. The capability of the process, also known as the voice of the process, defines the quality of the output the process *actually* produces. A primary aim of process improvement is to narrow or eliminate any gap between the requirements of the customer and the capability of the process.

The most important level of measurement is the outcome level. The outcome level determines customer satisfaction and is based on the attempt to measure the customer's total experience when using the output. All processes should be designed to achieve or contribute to customer satisfaction. Outcome measures depend on the actual use of the output. Unfortunately, meaningful outcome measures are the least frequently used.

Consider an IIA Insurance Company representative's experience regarding a request for a loss control inspection report (and a failure to receive it in a timely fashion), and these recommendations that can serve as an example to clarify the three levels of performance measurement. For example, one of the possible and relevant process measures is turnaround time, the amount of time that passes between an underwriter's request for an inspection report and recommendations and the underwriter's receipt of the report and recommendations. Based on the inability of the insurer's representative to obtain the report for the customer in a timely fashion, it seems clear that IIA had no turnaround-time process measures in place. Instead, requests were assigned on a first-come, first-served basis.

Outcome measures reflect the experience of the customer on using the output. For example, in order for the IIA insurance representative seeking the loss control report to be satisfied, he or she would have had to receive a report and recommendations that contained all the information needed to underwrite the business in time to meet the customer's requirements, the deadline set by the potential insured. In other words, *the IIA representative looked to use the output as the input of his or her own work process.* From the IIA representative's point of view, the delayed delivery of the report made it useless, **scrap** that need not have been produced at all. Consequently, the process is in need of improvement.

Scrap

An output that is not received and used by an identifiable individual.

The attempt to measure the performance of the loss control report process at three levels demonstrates that performance standards either were never established or that they were established with a total disregard for the customer. Furthermore, the process has not been designed for the purpose of achieving customer satisfaction. Once this situation is made clear, it becomes a blinding flash of the obvious. But countless processes in place in countless organizations have grown up with no thought given to their role in customer satisfaction at all. For this reason, to see "the obvious" often takes a good deal of effort. The six-step process improvement model is a tool for discovering "the obvious."

Step 4—Understanding Why

The first three steps in the process improvement model pave the way for a thorough understanding of the process. Understanding why a process operates in the way it does is often gained through brainstorming to identify as many potential causes of problems as possible and then winnowing the few identified causes that lead to the bulk of the problems.

Statistical analysis, based on such tools as the Pareto analysis, cause-and-effect analysis, histograms, and control charts, are aids to a deep and thorough understanding of processes. Continuous improvement advocate Joseph M. Juran helped in this effort by enunciating the **Pareto Principle**, a rule of thumb based on the findings of Vilfredo Pareto: "Eighty percent of the problems are due to twenty percent of the causes." A Japanese continuous improvement advocate, Kaoru Ishikawa, points out that symptoms—the earliest signs of problems—are not causes. Taking actions to treat or merely mask symptoms does nothing to cure the underlying disease. He advocates seeking out **root causes**. Cause-and-effect diagrams (also known as fishbone charts or Ishikawa diagrams) are tools for sorting out symptoms, causes, and root causes. W. Edwards Deming, perhaps the best known of the quality advocates, also contributed to the understanding of processes by his ideas on **variation**. Variations in process outputs have causes, Deming argued, that can be identified and classified. He distinguished between **common causes of variation** (causes that are inherent in a process and produce variations that are within predictable limits) and **special causes of variation** (causes that can be attributed to specific reasons or events and produce variations that are unpredictable). Both types of causes can be treated to improve process performance. Histograms and control charts help to identify causes of unwanted variation.

Some students of continuous improvement argue that these statistical methods, which grew out of manufacturing operations, are less useful for service businesses. For instance, variation can lead to customer dissatisfaction with a manufactured product. To satisfy service customers, however, processes might need to be flexible enough to produce outputs that will satisfy the unique needs of unique customers. In other words, service processes might need variation in outputs to achieve customer satisfaction.

Pareto Principle

This states that eighty percent of the problems are due to twenty percent of the causes.

Root cause

The real cause of an accident or problem and not just a symptom.

Variation

Inconsistencies in the attributes of output.

Common causes of variation

Common causes of variation are inherent in a process and produce variations with predictable limits.

Special causes of variation

Causes of variation that are attributed to specific reasons or events and produce unpredictable variations.

The aim is not to collect data for its own sake or to measure activities because they can be measured, but *to identify the causes of problems that, if treated, will provide the greatest improvement and increase customer satisfaction.*

Step 5—Developing and Testing Ideas

The six steps in the process improvement model tend to overlap, to be performed almost simultaneously. Before considering Step 5, briefly restating what the first four steps achieve is helpful.

Carrying out the first four steps in the process improvement model firmly defines the problem, establishes the process earmarked for improvement, measures how well it performs, and leads to an in-depth understanding of why it performs in that way—an identification and a sorting out of the fundamental causes of the most important problems. It would be almost impossible to gain this much detailed knowledge of a process without beginning to form ideas on how to improve the process, the fifth step in the model.

Understanding why a process operates in the way it does is achieved through a brainstorming session with a specific purpose and supported by data. The development of ideas on how to improve the performance of a process is often also achieved through brainstorming. The ideas generated on how to improve the process must also be sorted and evaluated in a search for the most effective solutions.

Discussion of the potential solutions can help evaluate them, but sometimes the ideas must actually be tested in advance of implementation. For instance, if customers complain about phone service, a team of customer service representatives (CSRs) might decide a new greeting would solve or minimize the problem. Use of the greeting by a few CSRs for a limited period of time before full implementation could test whether the new greeting achieves the intended result. Testing ideas can lead to a reconsideration of the work done in the earlier steps of the process improvement model. A potential solution, when tested, can raise a host of questions: Are the customers' requirements understood? Have the root causes of the problem been accurately identified? Has the process been fully documented?

Only when the owner or owners of the process are convinced that the best solution has been found can the final step in the model begin.

Step 6—Implementing and Evaluating Solutions

The sixth step in the model has two parts: (1) to implement the improvements selected in Step 5 and (2) to evaluate the improvements to ensure they achieve the desired aim. Evaluation necessarily includes documenting results. This evaluation in effect restarts the six steps in the process. The improvement—no matter how dramatic—must be viewed as a temporary one that will eventually be superseded. It is in this way that improvement becomes continuous. See the exhibit "Process Improvement Model Checklist."

Process Improvement Model Checklist

1. Define Problem
    - ❐ Identify output
    - ❐ Identify customers
    - ❐ Define requirements
    - ❐ Identify processes
    - ❐ Identify process owner

2. Identify and Document Process
    - ❐ Flowchart
    - ❐ Model
    - ❐ Identify participants

3. Measure Performance
    - ❐ Customer satisfaction
    - ❐ Customer requirements
    - ❐ Output delivered
    - ❐ Process parameters
    - ❐ Cost of quality

4. Understand Why
    - ❐ Distinguish major areas
    - ❐ Diagnose root causes
    - ❐ Understand variation
    - ❐ Common causes
    - ❐ Special causes
    - ❐ Capability

5. Develop and Test Ideas
    - ❐ Develop new ideas
    - ❐ Experiment
    - ❐ Test ideas to address root causes

6. Implement Solutions and Evaluate
    - ❐ Plan improvements
    - ❐ Implement system changes
    - ❐ Document system changes
    - ❐ Evaluate system performance
    - ❐ Evaluate six steps
    - ❐ Reward participants
    - ❐ Recycle to step 1

Adapted from Arthur R. Tenner and Irving S. DeToro, Total Quality Management, IIA Edition (Reading, Mass.: Addison-Wesley Publishing Company), p. 106. [DA04449]

DEFINING PROBLEMS IN TERMS OF THE PROCESS

Defining an organization's problems frequently involves restating specific objectives in terms of the relevant process. As a result, the organization can examine its problems not in terms of viewing them as one-time-only problems, each requiring a solution, but rather as part of a total process requiring varying solutions focused on quality improvement.

Some tools and rules are useful when carrying out the six steps of the process improvement model.[2] For example, restating specific objectives in terms of the process is often the approach needed to define a problem. Additionally, identifying and documenting the process is usually best carried out by developing a flowchart. Also, understanding why often requires the use of the Pareto Principle, the root cause analysis urged by Kaoru Ishikawa, or a study of the common and special causes of variation. These and other techniques provide a deep understanding of why a process performs in a certain way. See the exhibit "The Process Improvement Model."

The Process Improvement Model

The process improvement model is a set of six steps designed to be a guide to process improvement, not a rigid set of rules. These are the steps in the process improvement model:

1. Defining the problem in terms of the process

2. Identifying and documenting the process

3. Measuring performance

4. Understanding why

5. Developing and testing ideas

6. Implementing solutions and evaluating them, including the documentation of results

---

[DA04451]

Restating objectives in terms of the process enables organizations to consider various solutions to problems—rather than a single solution—that would have potentially remained invisible to management and staff without the redefinition and restatement of the problem. See the exhibit "Restating Problems in Terms of the Process."

Restating Problems in Terms of the Process

Results-Oriented Objective	Restate in Terms of the Process	Improvement
Expedite loss control report on the application submitted by ABC agency	Improve the process for producing loss control reports	Average turnaround time for *all* loss control reports reduced by 3 working days
Settle the Hotchkiss claim to avoid a court case	Improve the claim handling process	Average number of *all* claim cases going to court reduced by 18%
Recruit and train 2 new producers to increase sales	Improve the sales process	Sales increased by 6% with *no additions to staff*

[DA04456]

CUSTOMER VOICE AND PROCESS VOICE

Output measures in a process improvement model are established from two perspectives: the requirements of the customer and the capability of the process. These requirements are also known as the "voice of the customer" and the "voice of the process."

The voice of the customer in the process improvement model defines the quality of the output that the process should produce.[3] The voice of the process defines the quality of the output that the process actually produces. A primary aim of process improvement is to reduce or eliminate potential gaps between the requirements of the customer and the capability of the process. See the exhibit "The Process Improvement Model."

The Process Improvement Model

The process improvement model is a set of six steps designed to be a guide to process improvement, not a rigid set of rules. These are the steps in the process improvement model:

1. Defining the problem in terms of the process

2. Identifying and documenting the process

3. Measuring performance

4. Understanding why

5. Developing and testing ideas

6. Implementing solutions and evaluating them, including the documentation of results

[DA04457]

A primary aim of process improvement is to narrow or eliminate any gap between the requirements of the customer (customer voice) and the capability of the process (process voice). Output measures are descriptions of the output in terms of both the customer's requirements and the process's capability. For example, in the case of an IIA insurance company representative seeking a loss control report for his or her customer, the only customer requirement appears to be timeliness—a deadline. Underwriters might have many other requirements for loss control reports and recommendations. However, by using process improvement to narrow or eliminate gaps between the customer voice and process voice, IIA could have had a different result. IIA's process was designed without first determining the requirements of the customers—the customer's voice; therefore, the process is incapable of consistently producing outputs that meet even the single customer requirement, timeliness. The late delivery of the loss control report and recommendations constitutes the voice of the process rather than the voice of the customer.

PROCESS IMPROVEMENT MODEL CASE STUDY

The six-step process improvement model discussed in detail here reflects what many people have found to actually work in various settings.[4] It is an expansion of an approach to process improvement known as the P-D-C-A (plan-do-check-act) Cycle—also sometimes called the Shewhart or Deming cycle. Steps 1 to 4 in the process improvement model are equivalent to the "plan" phase of P-D-C-A. Step 5, the development and testing of ideas, accounts for the "do" and "check" phases of the **P-D-C-A Cycle**. Step 6 completes the cycle with "act" and simultaneously starts the cycle over again, the evaluation of the implemented improvement reinitiating the "plan" phase.

P-D-C-A Cycle

The P-D-C-A Cycle, also known as the Shewhart cycle and the Deming cycle, is an expansion of an approach to process improvement. The steps include Plan, Do, Check, and Act.

Karl Albrecht, in *The Only Thing That Matters*, argues that all businesses are "services" now that manufacturers also involve customers in the determination of output requirements. He emphasizes the customer orientation of continuous improvement, insisting that the voice of the customer is central to all considerations of process improvement. Albrecht says the purpose of process improvement is "to align all organizational systems and processes toward the ultimate purpose of delivering customer value." In keeping with this stated purpose, he offers three common-sense questions as a way to decide which processes are most blatantly in need of improvement. Those three questions are all based on the experiences of customers.

- Are there significant complaints, dissatisfaction, or demands to do better?
- Are there customer problems your system is neglecting, or even aggravating?
- Are there opportunities to add value for the customer, especially with minimum additional cost?

These three questions reflect a specific point of view—the point of view of someone who is responsible for all of an organization's processes.[5]

Albrecht, like many writers on continuous improvement, primarily addresses the top management teams of organizations. While it is true that the responsibility for continuous improvement must ultimately rest with the top management of an organization and cannot be effectively put in place without the commitment of top management, other points of view must be considered. Albrecht is aware of that and draws attention to three other points of view—that of (1) employees, (2) work groups, and (3) departments or organizations. From each point of view, the three questions he offers as a way of focusing on areas in need of improvement can be of value.

The various steps and recommendations in process improvement model should be followed when considering work scenarios relating to such topics as loss control, underwriting, service, and production. See the exhibit "The Process Improvement Model."

The Process Improvement Model

The process improvement model is a set of six steps designed to be a guide to process improvement, not a rigid set of rules. These are the steps in the process improvement model:

1. Defining the problem in terms of the process

2. Identifying and documenting the process

3. Measuring performance

4. Understanding why

5. Developing and testing ideas

6. Implementing solutions and evaluating them, including the documentation of results

[DA04457]

Process improvement is sometimes performed by the members of a work group with the guidance of the work group member who has been assigned ownership of the process. But processes do not operate in isolation. Instead, processes interconnect to form systems, that is, collections of processes. Systems can be confined to a single department or interconnect with the processes or systems of other departments or other organizations. Process improvement is viewed from a different perspective at each of these levels—the individual employee who is part of a work group; the work group as a whole, including the owner of the process; and the person responsible for a department's or an organization's systems.

Employees

Individual employees tend to view processes as tasks, the specific jobs they are responsible for performing directly themselves. Consider the perspective of a loss control specialist at an insurance company who is assigned the job of conducting an inspection and preparing a report and recommendations for a customer. The specialist is unaware of the customer's requirements and can only perform the assigned task well by preparing a report the department head would approve within a time limit the department head will find acceptable. The process of which the loss control specialist was a part was designed to achieve "boss satisfaction" rather than customer satisfaction—and in this case the two were not aligned. Nonetheless, the loss control specialist might adopt the routine of contacting the underwriter who requests an inspection before conducting the inspection. Processes can often be improved at the employee level through the way the employee decides to carry out the assigned task.

Work Groups

Work groups view process improvement from the perspective of the owner of the process. It takes in the interrelationships of specific jobs performed by individual employees. Usually, the work group's perspective emphasizes a single process, the group's way of contributing to a larger entity, the department or the organization. For example, the head of the loss control department at an insurance company that is having problems with its loss control reports could be tasked with being the owner of the loss control inspection process and given responsibility for its improvement. He or she could partner with staff and other managers as a work group, urging them to coordinate their efforts to contribute to the achievement of the company's underwriting and marketing goals. They would then be ideally positioned to satisfy their customers.

Departments or Organizations

From the point of view of a department or an organization, process improvement involves the coordination of a collection of processes, forming one or more systems. The emphasis from this perspective is on the ultimate contribution of the entire department or organization. Systems within a single department or organization can include cross-functional processes and require coordination from a broad perspective. For example, if an insurance company claims representative is frequently encountering the problem of obtaining policy information from another department, the problem should be reported to, for instance, the vice president of claims so that a continuous improvement program could begin.

SUMMARY

The process improvement model is a set of six steps designed to be a guide to process improvement, not a rigid set of rules. These are the steps in the process improvement model:

1. Defining the problem in terms of the process
2. Identifying and documenting the process
3. Measuring performance
4. Understanding why
5. Developing and testing ideas
6. Implementing solutions and evaluating them, including the documentation of results

These six steps represent a continuous cycle, with the evaluation of a solution in Step 6 providing the basis for redefining the problem in Step 1.

Restating specific objectives in terms of the process enables organizations to focus on quality improvement by considering varying alternatives from a more holistic viewpoint.

Output measures in a process improvement model are established based on the requirements of the customer (the customer's voice) and the capability of the process (the voice of the process).

Some specific tools and skills are necessary for people to engage in process improvement. Additionally, process improvement efforts inevitably influence organizational structures. The effects of process improvement efforts on an organization's daily activities can support quality improvement through employees, work groups, and the department and organization as a whole.

ASSIGNMENT NOTES

1. Adapted, in part, from Arthur R. Tenner and Irving J. DeToro, Total Quality Management, IIA Edition, (Reading, MA: Addison-Wesley, 1994), pp. 93–110.
2. Adapted, in part, from Arthur R. Tenner and Irving J. DeToro, Total Quality Management, IIA Edition, (Reading: MA: Addison-Wesley, 1994), pp. 93–110.
3. Adapted, in part, from Arthur R. Tenner and Irving J. DeToro, Total Quality Management, IIA Edition, (Reading: MA: Addison-Wesley, 1994), pp. 93–110.
4. Adapted, in part, from Arthur R. Tenner and Irving J. DeToro, Total Quality Management, IIA Edition, (Reading: MA: Addison-Wesley, 1994), pp. 93–110.
5. Karl Albrecht, The Only Thing That Matters (New York: Harper Collins, 1992), p. 159.

Direct Your Learning ▶▶

7

Process Improvement Tools

Educational Objectives

After learning the content of this assignment, you should be able to:

▶ Describe what can be achieved with data collection tools.

▶ Describe what can be achieved with data analysis tools.

▶ Given a case, recommend the appropriate process improvement tools.

▶ Describe the four dimensions of organizational performance.

Process Improvement Tools

DATA COLLECTION TOOLS

Collecting data is an important component of the process improvement model.

Before data can be analyzed in an attempt to understand why a process performs in the way it does, relevant data must be collected. A few common-sense, easy-to-use tools can be of great help in that effort:

- Complaint logs
- Moment-of-truth charts
- Change charts

Routine use of these tools can do much to replace opinions with data as the basis for making process improvement decisions.

Complaint Logs

A **complaint log** is merely a list of things customers complain about. It is a simple tool that can be used by anyone in an organization who is interested in increasing customer satisfaction. It is often most beneficial when used by customer service representatives (CSRs) or others who have frequent contact with customers. A complaint log might contain these types of complaints:

- Billing errors
- Unanswered phone calls
- Failure to return phone calls
- Inconvenient office hours
- High premium
- Dissatisfaction with claim service

The running list of complaints can be prioritized on the basis of frequency, cost, or importance to the customer. A review of the complaint log by an individual, a work group, a department, or an organization helps to keep the importance of customer orientation in mind and quickly focuses attention on problems and opportunities. Complaint logs are good starting points or triggers for the use of other techniques for understanding customers, such as assisting in the formulation of surveys, topics for focus groups or interviews, and so on. In addition, complaint logs provide raw data for further analysis.

Complaint log

A data collection tool that consists of a prioritized list of customer complaints.

Moment-of-Truth Charts

Moment of truth

Occurs when a customer makes contact with an organization.

A simple three-column **moment-of-truth** chart can be used to track the performance of an individual, a work group, a department, or an organization with respect to one specific moment of truth. An insurance agency might use such a chart to track performance at the time of renewal of policies, for instance.

The three columns of the chart are headed "negative," "expectations," and "positive." With each renewal of a policy, the chart is completed to show those elements in the transaction that failed to meet customer expectations, those elements that met customer expectations, and those elements that exceeded customer expectations. See the exhibit "Moment-of-Truth Chart: Policy Renewal."

Moment-of-Truth Chart: Policy Renewal

Negative	Expectations	Positive
Filling out forms	Convenience	Rapid phone follow-up on receipt of forms
Delayed delivery of policy	Prompt service	Small gift with apology for delay
Billing errors	Clear, error-free bills	Friendly CSR intervenes to correct errors

[DA04459]

Change Charts

Performance changes over time. These changes can go unnoticed unless efforts are made to track variables. The best way to track variables is by making a **change chart**.

Change chart

A data collection tool that tracks performance over time and is useful when one performance variable has been spotted as a potential problem or when testing ideas for process improvement.

The chart consists of two lines or axes, one for the performance variable being traced and the other for the period of time being considered. The change chart is most useful when one performance variable has been spotted as a potential problem or when testing ideas for process improvement. Complaints about billing errors, for instance, might occur with such frequency that it is decided to track those complaints for a three-month period. See the exhibit "Change Chart: Billing Errors."

The production of a change chart indicates a slight but steady increase in complaints about billing errors over a three-month period. The change chart indicates that the billing process needs attention and should be considered a candidate for process improvement.

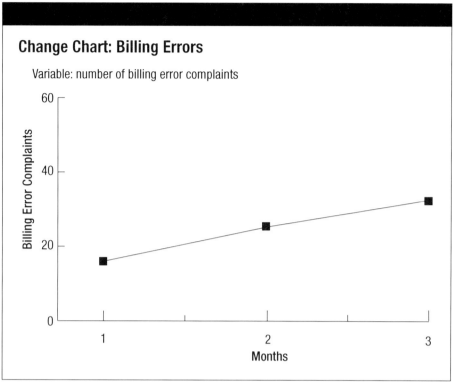

Change Chart: Billing Errors

Variable: number of billing error complaints

[DA04460]

Adapting and Combining Tools

Data collection tools can be adapted for a variety of purposes. In addition, they are often most effective when they are used in combination. Patrick Allnutt found that in one week, the members of his personal auto data entry team set aside 100 incomplete applications for various reasons:

- Seventy-three lacked signatures.
- Twelve lacked information on past accidents.
- Six gave no deductible amount.
- Five did not provide the applicant's age.
- Four did not give the distance driven to and from work.

How did he collect this data?

Patrick could have adapted the complaint log to an incomplete information log, simply requesting team members to note the reasons for setting aside incomplete applications. At the end of a week, Patrick would then be in a position to total the types of information missing from the applications.

Now suppose Patrick sent a letter to agents to remind them of the need to submit signed applications. In the letter, he pointed out that receipt of signed applications would decrease the time it takes to process applications, improving service for the agents and their clients. To determine the effectiveness of the letter, Patrick might ask team members to continue maintaining their logs for a three-month period. In this case, Patrick would not only total the types of information missing from applications but also use the weekly logs to construct a change chart for unsigned applications. See the exhibit "Change Chart: Unsigned Applications."

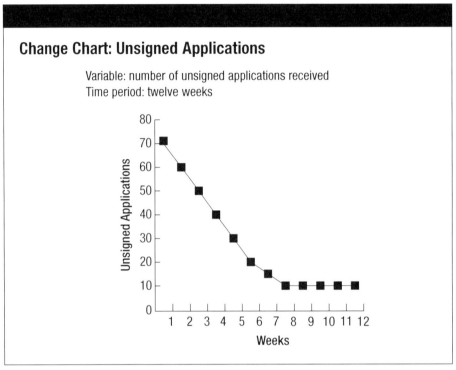

Change Chart: Unsigned Applications

Variable: number of unsigned applications received
Time period: twelve weeks

[DA04461]

The chart could be used to demonstrate to team members and others that the letter to agents had helped to solve the problem but had not yet eliminated it.

However, Patrick could have analyzed the data collected in the logs in another way by adapting the moment-of-truth chart. Suppose the data entered by his team are used by the personal auto underwriting department. The underwriting of personal auto applications has been automated, with underwriters personally considering applications only on an exception basis, that is, they review only those applications that the computer determines are neither clearly acceptable nor clearly unacceptable. Each contact between Patrick's team and the personal auto underwriting department constitutes a moment of truth.

The construction of a moment-of-truth chart could lead to a clearer understanding of the underwriting department's expectations and how to best meet them. For instance, it might be discovered that applications without signatures can be processed, rather than set aside, as long as the agent or prospective policyholder is notified of the absent signature. However, accident information, age of the applicant, and the distance driven to and from work are critical underwriting factors, and applications without this information should continue to be set aside. Finally, applications that lack a requested deductible amount could be processed and the deductible negotiated only if the company decides to write the business. In this way, Patrick and his team would learn that all incomplete applications need not be treated in the same way, establishing new procedures.

DATA ANALYSIS TOOLS

Several tools can be used for understanding how a process performs:

- Cause-and-effect analysis
- Pareto analysis
- Histograms
- Control charts

Understanding why a process performs in the way it does calls for brainstorming, collecting data, and analyzing data. Distinguishing among these three activities is not always possible or even desirable. They tend to overlap.

Cause-and-Effect Analysis

Cause-and-effect analysis is associated with Kaoru Ishikawa and his emphasis on finding and treating the root causes of problems. The analysis consists of the collective preparation of a **fishbone diagram** by a group. The diagram is a tool for focusing the efforts of a group while brainstorming the possible causes of a problem, leading the group to the discovery of the root cause or causes of the problem.

The diagram itself is constructed by the leader of the group by recording the responses of members of the group to questions. The diagram is shaped like a fish. The problem—that is, the effect—is written at the extreme right, at the nose of the fish. The broad categories of possible causes of the problem are listed as the "bones" of the fish. (Broad categories of causes vary but often include such things as procedures, people, and equipment.)

One variation on this approach is for the steps in a process, rather than the broad categories of possible causes of a problem, to serve as the bones of the diagram. In either case, the group completes the diagram by repeatedly asking and answering the question, "Why does this happen?" The question is raised, and the group's answers are recorded until the group can think of no more causes. See the exhibit "Fishbone Diagram: Bad Faith Lawsuit."

Cause-and-effect analysis
An analytical tool that uses fishbone diagrams to reveal root causes of problems.

Fishbone diagram
An analytical tool that records all possible causes of problems that a group can think of during a brainstorming session to find and treat root causes of problems.

Fishbone Diagram: Bad Faith Lawsuit

Effect

Bad Faith Lawsuit

Inadequate monitoring

Confused lines of authority

Confrontational tactics

Failure to understand sources of negotiating power

Improper workload

Supervision

Uninformed about litigation alternatives

Negotiation

Poor telephone skills

Inadequate written communication

Failure to anticipate bad faith potential

Communications and Human Relations

Poor listening

Poor stress management

Inadequate investigation

Inaccurate damage evaluation

Lack of knowledge of unfair claim practices

Claim Knowledge and Technical Skills

Causes

[DA04462]

Pareto Analysis

The Pareto rule states, "Eighty percent of the problems are the result of twenty percent of the causes." The Pareto analysis is a way to determine which causes of problems to tackle and a way to identify those relatively few causes of problems that, if corrected, offer the greatest potential for improvement. A Pareto analysis consists of three phases:

1. Study
2. Graph
3. Interpret

An example can help clarify these three phases. Suppose Insure-All became aware of problems with the way it handles claims and the claim vice president formed a team and charged it with improving the company's claim-handling process. The team members might begin by requesting customer service representatives (CSRs) and inside claim handlers to maintain complaint logs. The data collected in these logs would provide the team with a list of complaints. These complaints identify the causes of the problems to be solved.

Analysis of the causes of problems depends on the determination of a unit of measurement. The most common units of measurement are frequency and cost. For instance, Insure-All's claim-handling improvement team might reasonably decide that frequency is the appropriate unit of measure. In that case, the number of complaints received about each cause would be the basis for determining the relative importance of the various causes. A time period for the study must also be determined in advance. The study phase of a Pareto analysis results in a list of possible causes. See the exhibit "Complaint Log: Claims Received Between 9/1 and 12/1."

Complaint Log: Claims Received Between 9/1 and 12/1

Denial of coverage	1
Rudeness	11
Unresponsiveness	16
Broken appointments	3
Stalling	5
Unfair payment	4
Insensitive	3
Total	43

The data in Insure-All's complaint log can then be used to draw a bar graph. The graph consists of two lines or axes, one horizontal and one vertical. The identified causes are placed along the horizontal axis. The units of measurement (in this case, frequency) are placed along the vertical axis. See the exhibit "Bar Graph: Claim Complaints."

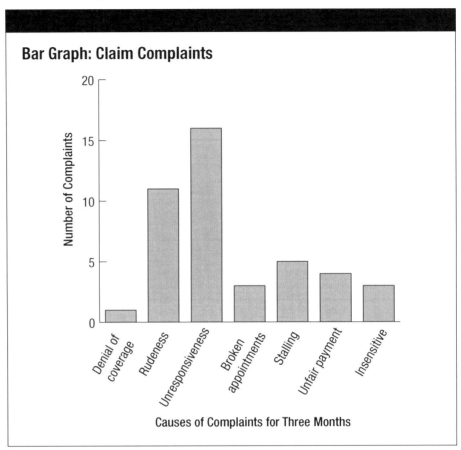

Bar Graph: Claim Complaints

[DA04467]

Although it is a simple matter to draw the bar graph, doing so should be treated as an opportunity for further analysis by raising questions about the data and rethinking the approach.

For instance, based on Pareto analysis, the Insure-All team could easily conclude that "unresponsiveness" and "rudeness" should be tackled in order to improve the company's claim-handling process. It would be hard to argue against that conclusion, based on the data collected and organized to carry out the Pareto analysis. Eliminating those problems would certainly decrease the number and frequency of customer complaints. But as students of risk management long ago learned, relying on a single measurement (frequency, in this case) can produce misleading results by ignoring severity. In other words, the costs involved in each complaint should perhaps be considered, too. A single denial of coverage could lead to an exceedingly expensive lawsuit, publicly discussed, with a far-reaching and long-lasting influence on Insure-All's reputation. By comparison, the relatively frequent complaints about "unresponsiveness" and "rudeness" could be passing annoyances, rapidly forgotten or offset by other aspects of the company's service. These frequent complaints should not be ignored; however, to understand the relatively few important causes of the company's claim-handling problems, the team might need to perform two Pareto analyses, one with frequency as the unit of measure and the other with cost as the unit of measure.

The interpretation phase of a Pareto analysis can be carried out once the bar graph has been prepared. The tallest bar often indicates the most important cause. Caution must still be exercised, however. At the interpretation phase, the unit of measurement that has been selected becomes crucial.

Histograms

Histograms assist in the analysis of the capability of a process, as well as aiding in the identification of causes of problems. In a way, they convert collected data on the voice of the process to a usable form so that analysis can take place and then a problem can be recognized.

For instance, Insure-All uses logs to track the amount of time it takes to reach underwriting decisions on commercial risks. Carrie Uhlman, a commercial underwriting manager, uses the data from the logs as the basis for calculations to prepare a histogram using a bar graph format. The varying amounts of the unit of measure, in this case working days, are displayed along the horizontal axis. The frequency counts are displayed along the vertical axis. See the exhibit "Histogram: Time for Underwriting Decisions."

Histograms differ from some other analytical tools in that they reflect data that has been grouped. In this case, the bars represent classes of data, ranges of working days.

One way to interpret histograms is to determine the difference between the voice of the process and the voice of the customer. If research shows that agents, brokers, or commercial lines customers expect underwriting decisions to be made in ten to fifteen working days, for example, lines drawn through the histogram graphically demonstrate how the voice of the process exceeds or fails to meet customer expectations. The histogram, in this way, also helps to establish the variation of the process.

> **Histogram**
>
> A plot of a distribution of observations with the horizontal axis representing the class intervals and the vertical axis representing the frequency or probability of outcomes.

Control Charts

Control charts also assist in the study of variation. The main purpose of control charts is to monitor and control processes through the study of variation over time and its source. W. Edwards Deming made a distinction between common causes of variation and special causes of variation. Common causes of variation are inherent to the process, arising from the very nature of the process, the combination of people, material, machinery, procedures, environment, and so on that make up the process. Special causes of variation come from outside the process as it is routinely constituted.

> **Control chart**
>
> Used to demonstrate the variation in a process and to determine whether the variation is the result of common or special causes.

Histogram: Time for Underwriting Decisions

[DA04468]

The route usually taken to work can be seen as a process that operates routinely but with variations arising from common causes. Traffic lights will be red at times and green at other times. Traffic might move more slowly than usual on rainy days. The traffic lights and road conditions are common causes of variation. However, a road closed by flooding following a hurricane represents a special cause of variation. Studying both the common and the special causes of variation can help in process improvement. In general, improvement of a process that displays common cause variation requires studying the process. For instance, the route to work might be improved by resurfacing roads to diminish their slickness on rainy days. Generally, improvement of a process that displays special cause variation requires studying the specific incident, in this case, the flooding that closed the road. Establishing a satisfactory alternative route for those rare occasions might be a way of treating this special cause of variation.

Sam Bryan, the owner of Independence Insurance Agency, uses control charts as one of the ways he analyzes his book of business. Sam specializes in personal auto insurance and therefore wants to stay well aware of the auto claims his book of business generates.

Sam has prepared a control chart based on the number of auto claims generated by his clients on a monthly basis for a two-year period. This chart displays no special causes of variation. The number of claims per month never exceeds the upper control limit (UCL). It is "statistically stable" because it displays only common causes of variation. If improvement is needed or desired, it should result from a study of the process. See the exhibit "Auto Claims Control Chart: Common Causes of Variation."

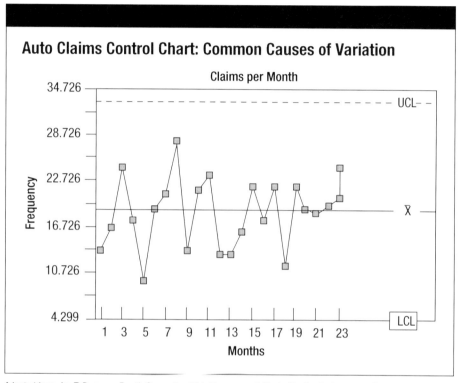

Auto Claims Control Chart: Common Causes of Variation

Adapted from Jay T. Deragon, Fourth Generation Risk Management (Nashville: Quality Insurance Congress, 1995). [DA04469]

Two years later, Sam prepares a second control chart. This one, however, displays a special cause of variation. The number of claims in month twenty exceeds the UCL, indicating a special cause of variation. Determining the special cause and how it might be prevented or minimized in the future should result from a study of the incident itself. (Perhaps a hail storm caused the sharp increase in reported auto claims.) See the exhibit "Auto Claims Control Chart: Special Cause of Variation."

In both cases, control charts permit Sam Bryan to monitor the auto claims generated by his book of business and, when necessary or desirable, concentrate on either the process itself or an unusual incident to improve future performance.

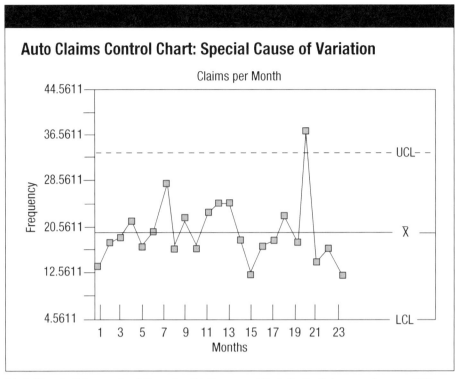

Auto Claims Control Chart: Special Cause of Variation

Adapted from Jay T. Deragon, Fourth Generation Risk Management (Nashville: Quality Insurance Congress, 1995). [DA04472]

PROCESS IMPROVEMENT TOOLS CASE STUDY

Process improvement tools range from the simple to the sophisticated and from the easy-to-use to those that can be used effectively only after some training and practice.

A process improvement case study is provided, based on the actual experiences of an insurance company that tried to improve its underwriting process. Process improvement is most effective in organizations that desire and respect employee involvement.

Improving the Underwriting Process at Insurespec

Insurespec is a specialized insurance company that has been in business for a little more than fifteen years. The company started with an idea, the founder's conviction that large manufacturing firms have specialized insurance and risk management needs that could be better met than they then were. He built the business around the idea that customers—agents, brokers, and clients— determine quality. He also rapidly expanded so that Insurespec, known as Double-Eye, consists of three related organizations: II Underwriting, II Loss Control, and II Claims. The result is that Insurespec offers a range of services while focusing on a narrow target market with very specific needs.

A Page From the History of Quality

In recent years, many executives have heard about the benefits other organizations have achieved through the application of "Six Sigma" statistical techniques for process improvement.

The term sigma (a Greek letter) comes from the discipline of statistics and is used to describe variation. One of the aims of continuous improvement efforts is to limit variation of results so that customers can expect the same quality of service all of the time.

Six Sigma equates statistically to 3.4 defects per million. The purpose of Six Sigma is to measure defects or failures and design or improve processes so that defects do not exceed this high standard. The heart of Six Sigma can be said to come from Philip B. Crosby's "zero defects" programs, but the brains of Six Sigma more closely resemble the work of Walter Shewhart, W. Edwards Deming, and Joseph Juran, who used statistics and quantitative techniques to diagnose and solve process problems.

The Six Sigma technique originated at Motorola in the early 1990s. Following Motorola's success, other companies such as General Electric, Sony, and Allied Signal espoused Six Sigma techniques. A Six Sigma initiative in an organization is designed to change the corporate culture by focusing on inventive ways to achieve the aggressive 3.4 defects-per-million goal.

Jack Welch, former CEO of General Electric (GE), describes Six Sigma as the most challenging and potentially rewarding initiative ever undertaken at GE. The GE annual reports state that Six Sigma delivers hundreds of millions of dollars to GE's operating income each year. The initiative has also been introduced into GE-owned insurance and reinsurance organizations.

[DA04475]

This organizational structure grew up in part as a result of a formal quality initiative that began ten years ago. Surveys and focus groups showed that clients were interested in loss control inspections and recommendations and claim services separately from the purchase of insurance. The formation of II Loss Control and II Claims resulted from this identification of a widespread customer need. Both organizations have been highly successful.

II Underwriting also remained successful but, in time, began to lose some long-standing accounts to competitors. About two years ago, Insurespec launched a continuous improvement effort focusing specifically on the underwriting process.

A ten-member team consisting of the underwriting vice president, selected underwriting managers, underwriters, underwriting assistants, the quality assurance officer, and two consultants was formed and charged with developing an underwriting process improvement strategy.

The team decided to first establish objectives and then come up with recommended ways to achieve those objectives. Top management's agreement on the objectives and recommendations would be sought before implementing any recommended changes.

The team determined the objectives on the basis of feedback over a two-year period from agents, brokers, clients, prospective clients, and former clients, who had chosen to take their business elsewhere. The team drafted these objectives:

- Streamline the underwriting process
- Improve productivity
- Reduce cycle time
- Improve quality

To come up with recommendations for improvements that would meet these objectives, the team decided to take this approach:

1. Document current process
2. Identify non-value-added activities from the customer perspective
3. Determine root causes for non-value-added activities
4. Develop recommendations to eliminate or minimize non-value-added activities
5. Document future process
6. Develop implementation plan
7. Identify performance measures to monitor implementation

At this point, the ten-member team divided into two teams. Six members became a process team, and four members became a project steering committee, serving as a resource to the process team and providing the process team with a link to the organization's top management.

The Current Process

Documenting the process was a learning experience. Although all of the team members, except the consultant, were very familiar with some aspects of the process, none of them had ever considered the process in its entirety.

In the end, team members concluded the process could be described as a sequence of five major steps, each step taking in a number of operations. The team drew a map of the current process. See the exhibit "Current Underwriting Process."

The Approach

Ursula Andrews, an underwriter who had been named leader of the process team, presented team members with a proposed approach for them to take based on the overall strategy that had been determined, the mapped current process, and her own sense of the amount of time team members could devote

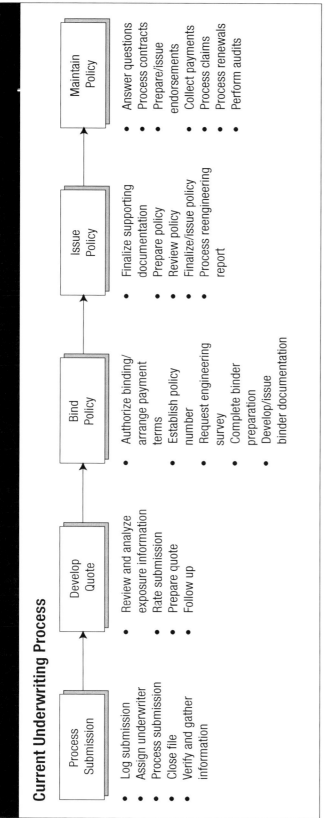

Current Underwriting Process

Process Submission
- Log submission
- Assign underwriter
- Process submission
- Close file
- Verify and gather information

Develop Quote
- Review and analyze exposure information
- Rate submission
- Prepare quote
- Follow up

Bind Policy
- Authorize binding/arrange payment terms
- Establish policy number
- Request engineering survey
- Complete binder preparation
- Develop/issue binder documentation

Issue Policy
- Finalize supporting documentation
- Prepare policy
- Review policy
- Finalize/issue policy
- Process reengineering report

Maintain Policy
- Answer questions
- Process contracts
- Prepare/issue endorsements
- Collect payments
- Process claims
- Process renewals
- Perform audits

[DA04476]

to the project and how they would most profitably work together. She urged that each member, working independently, come up with a list of non-value-added activities from the perspective of the customer and then e-mail the lists to her. She would combine and refine the lists. The team would then work together as a group, meeting weekly, to decide on which non-value-added activities to tackle, to determine the root causes of those activities, and to ultimately develop recommendations to eliminate or minimize non-value-added activities. See the exhibit "Minimization of Non-Value-Added Activities."

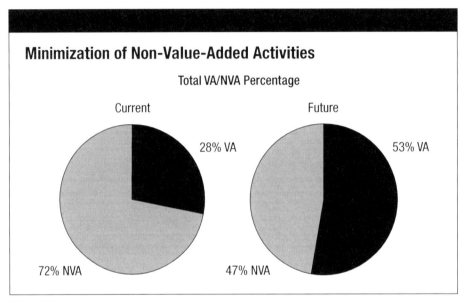

Minimization of Non-Value-Added Activities

Total VA/NVA Percentage

Current — 28% VA, 72% NVA

Future — 53% VA, 47% NVA

[DA04480]

The Recommendations

After several weeks, the process team had established some recommendations and plotted a proposed new process. The process team met with the project steering committee to review the recommendations and the potential benefits of implementing the proposed new process. Discussions resulted in eliminating a few recommendations and slightly modifying the proposed new process. The team and the committee then prepared several graphics to make the benefits of the recommendations clear to the top management team and co-workers.

The projected cycle time improvement can be placed in a Cycle Time Comparison chart. See the exhibit "Cycle Time Comparison."

A chart can illustrate the projected productivity improvement. See the exhibit "Productivity Comparison."

Top management accepted the proposals and sketched an implementation plan. The plan was announced by the president and CEO of Insurespec, who

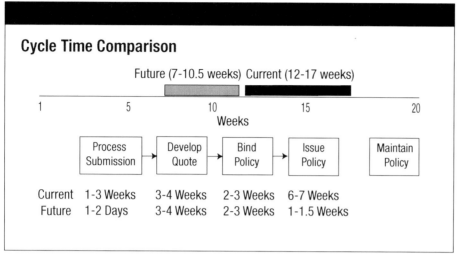

Cycle Time Comparison

Future (7-10.5 weeks) Current (12-17 weeks)

Weeks

	Process Submission	Develop Quote	Bind Policy	Issue Policy	Maintain Policy
Current	1-3 Weeks	3-4 Weeks	2-3 Weeks	6-7 Weeks	
Future	1-2 Days	3-4 Weeks	2-3 Weeks	1-1.5 Weeks	

[DA04477]

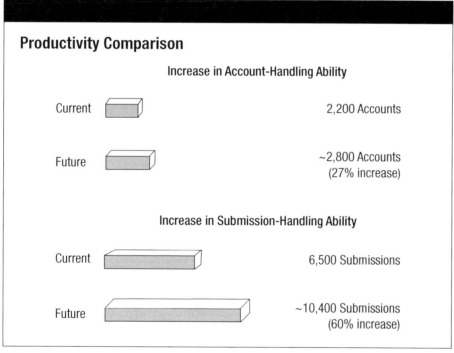

Productivity Comparison

Increase in Account-Handling Ability

Current — 2,200 Accounts

Future — ~2,800 Accounts (27% increase)

Increase in Submission-Handling Ability

Current — 6,500 Submissions

Future — ~10,400 Submissions (60% increase)

[DA04479]

began by saying that he was proud of the achievement of the process improvement team. He went on to say this:

> The recommendations of the team will change the way we think and the way we work. Some tasks will be eliminated, others altered beyond recognition. But no people will be lost as a result of these changes. There will be a need for training, for learning new skills, and for taking on new responsibilities. But we will increase customer satisfaction, cut our cycle time, and improve our productivity with no reduction in staff. For us, continuous improvement is a win-win situation. Now let's celebrate. The future looks brighter for all of us, thanks to the work of the underwriting process improvement team.

MEASURING ORGANIZATIONAL PERFORMANCE

Organizational performance cannot be measured on the basis of process analysis alone. Measurement should account for all of an organization's stakeholders.

Organizational performance must be measured in four dimensions, including but not limited to financial measures. These four dimensions represent an organization's various stakeholders and emphasize that customer satisfaction parallels employee job satisfaction and the satisfaction of members of the community in which the organization resides.

The process improvement tools provide ways to make invisible figures visible. But the visible figures—financial figures—cannot be ignored. In fact, the performance of an organization must be measured in four dimensions, expanding the definition of customers to include all **stakeholders**, that is, (1) customers in the sense of end-users of products or services, (2) financial stakeholders (owners, principals, shareholders, managers, in some cases policyholders, and so on), (3) employees, and (4) the community in which the organization operates (regulators, governments, neighbors, and so on). The four dimensions for measuring organizational performance can be displayed graphically. See the exhibit "Four Dimensions for Measuring Organizational Performance."

Stakeholder

Anyone with a financial interest in the corporation.

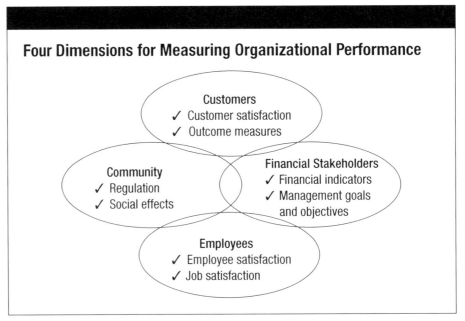

[DA04481]

By considering all stakeholders, organizations can analyze the outcomes of organizational processes in the broadest sense, not only the outcomes experienced by customers who directly receive the outputs. An organization's outputs include the financial return derived, the visible figures; the job satisfaction derived by employees, a mirror image of customer satisfaction and necessarily bound up with it; and the social effect of an organization's operations.

SUMMARY

The routine use of data collection tools can do much to help people understand the work processes they engage in and to discover ways of improving them.

Tools have been developed to assist in the analysis of data. These include cause-and-effect analyses, Pareto analyses, histograms, and control charts. These tools can be adapted for use in a wide variety of situations and are often most effective when used in combination.

The Insurespec case provides an example of process improvement in action in a fictional insurance company setting. The case demonstrates the kinds of things process improvement can achieve. It also shows how process improvement might fit in with an insurance organization's structure. One of the difficulties with process improvement is the need to continue to work within a current process while analyzing that process and planning to change it.

Performance of organizations must be measured in four dimensions, considering all stakeholders in the organization: (1) customers, (2) financial stakeholders, (3) employees, and (4) the community in the broadest sense.

Direct Your Learning ▶▶

8

Leadership, Teamwork, and Organizational Structures

Educational Objectives

After learning the content of this assignment, you should be able to:

▷ Distinguish between leadership and management.

▷ Distinguish among a mission statement; vision statement; and statement of values, goals, and objectives.

▷ Describe the three elements required for employee empowerment as well as the difference between compliance and commitment.

▷ Describe the four stages of team development.

▷ Explain why organizational structures vary.

Leadership, Teamwork, and Organizational Structures

LEADERSHIP AND MANAGEMENT

As you study leadership, think of ways that you can use its primary roles and outlook on the job.

Organizations that are dedicated to meeting the changing needs of customers can only hope to do so if they have employees who are involved, satisfied, and dedicated. The development of such a staff requires leadership.

Although leadership must be displayed by an organization's senior management for continuous improvement efforts to succeed, its primary roles are not limited to executives. The development of an energetic, responsible, involved work force takes leadership.

Leadership and **management** are important to an organization. One of the lessons that has been learned about efforts at continuous improvement is that they often end in disappointment and frustration if they lack a firm, consistent, knowledgeable commitment from the organization's senior management. Most importantly, this commitment cannot be a matter of mere words. After all, how many business executives are likely to publicly state that they are opposed to customer satisfaction, employee job satisfaction, or continuous improvement?

The commitment must be demonstrated, day in and day out, through deeds and decisions. Leadership, as it is used here, might be defined as the ability and willingness to consistently demonstrate a commitment to continuous improvement. Defined in this way, leadership differs from management. In some ways, they appear to be opposites. They are in fact different but related functions.

The aim of leadership in the workplace is the improvement of systems, collections of related processes. The aim of management is to achieve results. These aims require different skills, activities, and views of the nature of work and the workplace. The traditionally defined functions of management are (1) plan, (2) organize, (3) direct, (4) coordinate, and (5) control. The required roles of leadership have been called (1) envision, (2) align, (3) empower, (4) coach, and (5) care. These functions and roles can be displayed graphically. See the exhibit "Management Functions Versus Leadership Functions."

Warren Bennis, author of the book *Why Leaders Can't Lead*, has summed up the difference between leadership and management this way: "Leaders are people who do the right things; managers are people who do things right."

Leadership

A function of continuous improvement with the aim of improving systems.

Management

The set of functions, including planning, organizing, leading, and controlling resources, that enable organizations to achieve their goals efficiently and effectively.

Management Functions Versus Leadership Functions

Functions of Management	Roles of Leadership
Plan	Envision
Organize	Align
Direct	Empower
Coordinate	Coach
Control	Care

Aim of Management	Aim of Leadership
Achieve Results	Improve Systems

[DA04482]

Even if this distinction has limitations—there is little value in doing the right things wrong or in doing the wrong things right—it helps clarify the difference between an emphasis on what to do and an emphasis on how to do it. Continuous improvement requires both leadership and management. Continuous improvement advocates recognize the need to make the role of leadership at least equal in importance to that of the management function. The result is the growing realization that what is done and the way it is accomplished are of equal importance. In practice, this often translates into the need for leadership by example, again emphasizing deeds and decisions rather than words.

Organizations now often draw attention to this shifting emphasis by raising fundamental questions about the nature and purpose of the organization. In some cases, the answers to these questions serve as the basis for public statements. Some of the questions are these:

* What is our purpose? (mission)
* What do we want to become? (vision)
* How do we want to act? (values)
* What must be done in the short term (objectives) and the long term (goals) to fulfill the mission and move toward the vision?

Of primary concern to leaders is how the organization's mission, vision, values, goals, and objectives connect with customers.

AN ORGANIZATION'S PUBLIC STATEMENTS

Drafting or revising mission statements; vision statements; and statements of values, goals, and objectives can be a valuable exercise for organizations.

Of primary concern to leaders is how the organization's **mission**, **vision**, **values**, **goals**, and **objectives** connect with customers.

Mission

Organizations tend to take their purpose for granted. Nonetheless, when the question is seriously considered, differing opinions often emerge. The benefits of discussing the issue, agreeing on it, and reducing the mission to writing in a mission statement are that doing so (1) clarifies the nature of the organization, (2) provides guidance for decision making, (3) builds consensus, and (4) consciously gives employees the ability to identify with the mission. It is difficult to operate with a sense of purpose if that purpose remains vague, unknown, or unstated. See the exhibit "Sample Mission Statement."

Sample Mission Statement

Our company is committed to providing financial protection to our policyholders by delivering quality property and casualty products and services through the independent agency system.

We will seek increased efficiencies through the sharing of core support services and maintain responsiveness by staying close to our markets in claims, marketing, and underwriting. We will pursue profitable growth through our existing regional companies and through acquisitions.

The foundation of this approach is a recognition that employees and agents are our most valuable assets. Their success is the key to achieving our mission.

[DA04386]

Vision

A vision is simply a broad statement that describes how the organization intends to look in the future. It recognizes that organizations change over time and provides a concrete picture of the future state the organization wishes to attain. In this way, it is necessarily related to the mission, the current purpose of the organization, but is not limited to that. It provides a long-range target that the organization should eventually hit by fulfilling the current mission. For example, a vision statement might read: "During the next decade, we want to become the preferred provider of personal lines property-casualty insurance in the United States."

Many people within an organization can have alternative visions of its future. Openly discussing the vision, building consensus on it, and writing it down further clarify the nature of the organization, offer a guide for day-to-day decisions and operations, and consciously offer employees a concrete future to work toward. A vision, if shared, is a focal point for uniting the individuals that make up an organization, a way for them to be bound together not only for the present but also over time.

Vision
An idea of what an organization wants to become.

Mission
An organization's purpose.

Goal
A high-level organizational aspiration usually associated with strategy.

Values
An organization's values reflect its sense of acceptable ways of doing business.

Objectives
Short-term intentions necessary to achieve goals.

Values

Just as all organizations have a current purpose and an idea of the future, whether or not these are stated and publicly discussed, all organizations have a sense of acceptable ways of doing business. Left unstated, these acceptable ways of doing business remain vague (sending mixed signals to customers, suppliers, neighbors, and employees) and must be deduced by employees based on their observations of the behavior of co-workers and the responses to that behavior. Stating these acceptable ways of doing business, the kinds of behavior the organization wants to exhibit, can help clear the air.

Unacceptable behavior is then clearly understood by all. A statement of an organization's values is usually most helpful if it is brief, clear, and related to performing the current mission and striving for the long-term vision. One of W. Edwards Deming's "fourteen points" calls on leaders of and within organizations to drive out fear, create a climate of trust, and develop an environment that welcomes innovation. A statement of values, if acted on and supported consistently, can help organizational leaders accomplish these things. For example, Progressive Corporation's statement of core values reads: "We respect all people, value the differences among them and deal with them in a way we want to be dealt with; this requires us to know ourselves and to try and understand others."[1]

Goals and Objectives

Goals translate an organization's mission and vision into broad, long-term intentions. Objectives spell out the interim, incremental steps that must be taken within specific time periods to achieve goals.

Objectives answer the questions how much? of what? and by when? Both goals and objectives focus on what should be done, a matter of leadership. How the goals and objectives should be achieved—doing things right—is a matter of management, calling for action plans, resource allocation, training when needed, and so on. An organization can consider the strategic objectives of other organizations and competitors before selecting its own strategic objectives. See the exhibit "Sample Strategic Objectives."

Preparation of Statements

One person's vision might be another person's nightmare. The idea that mission statements, vision statements, values, goals, objectives, and similar statements can be written by a single individual or a senior management team, operating in a vacuum, and then printed and posted with the expectation that employees will be inspired by them is at best silly and at worst cynical. The very way the statements are prepared can encourage or undercut their ability to increase employee involvement—a primary reason for drafting the statements. Employees should become involved in the preparation of the statements long before they are printed or posted. In fact, it may be that they

Sample Strategic Objectives

Financial

- Meet stakeholders' expectations
- Achieve profitable growth
- Improve operating performance
- Ensure consistent reserve adequacy

Customer

- Improve market share
- Satisfy agents
- Satisfy policyholders

Internal Processes

- Improve agency management
- Optimize underwriting effectiveness and policy processing
- Optimize claim-handling processes
- Develop responsive pricing

Innovation and Learning

- Align training with performance and business needs
- Promote high-performing work force
- Provide an environment that fosters innovation
- Effectively integrate and disseminate innovation

[DA04483]

never will be printed and posted but merely maintained as works-in-progress that can be revisited and revised in the future. What Peter Senge says about visions in his book *The Fifth Discipline* can be applied to all of the types of statements associated with organizational leadership:

> Visions that are truly shared take time to emerge. They grow as a byproduct of interactions of individual visions. Experience suggests that visions that are genuinely shared require ongoing conversation where individuals not only feel free to express their dreams, but also learn how to listen to each other's dreams. Out of this listening, new insights into what is possible gradually emerge.[2]

One sign of leadership is the ability to raise fundamental questions about an organization without rushing to answer them, the ability to listen carefully to what others—employees, suppliers, customers—say in response to these questions. Raising the questions and taking an interest in the possible answers help to establish an atmosphere conducive to continuous improvement. This does not relieve an organization's management of its responsibility for determining the organization's direction and establishing its policies, strategies, and processes. It simply recognizes that employees are more likely to support the direction, policies, strategies, processes, and systems if they have helped to influence or shape them. This is as true for a department or function as it is for an organization.

Leadership and management, as discussed here, apply most readily to an organization's senior executives. Without the knowledgeable, consistent commitment of senior management, continuous improvement efforts tend to be at best limited and at worst destructive. Nonetheless, the approach for senior management described here—the emphasis on leadership rather than management, the need to involve employees in discussions of the organization's mission and vision, the need to align the efforts of everyone in the organization—can and should be reflected throughout the organization. One of the ways this happens is through the use of teams. See the exhibit "A Page From the History of Quality."

A Page From the History of Quality

You seldom improve quality by cutting costs, but you can often cut costs by improving quality.
— Karl Albrecht

One sign of the growing interest in continuous improvement in the insurance business is the formation, in 1992, of the Independent Insurance Agents of America (IIAA) Commission to Enhance Agency Value. The mission and vision statements of the commission clearly recognize the relationship between quality and value.

The mission statement reads:

To provide the leadership and tools for continuous quality improvement in agency-company operations and relationships in order to:

- Exceed customer expectations

- Enhance agency value

- Strengthen agency/company market share

The vision statement reads: "Successful agents and companies will use Best Practices Tools and Philosophies as an integral part of their businesses."

To fulfill its mission and strive toward achievement of its vision, the commission, beginning in 1993, in conjunction with Reagan & Associates and the Westinghouse Productivity and Quality Center, conducted a study, *The Best Practices in the Leading Independent Insurance Agencies in the U.S.* Since then, the study has been conducted annually and has led to the offering of seminars and the development of tools designed to continuously improve agency performance.

One unique aspect of this initiative is that it has made continuous improvement efforts a common ground for agencies and companies, recognizing the need to solve cross-functional and multi-organizational problems if continuous improvement efforts are to result in the delivery of quality insurance service, that is, if they are to achieve customer satisfaction.

The search for Best Practices represents a wide-scale benchmarking effort in the insurance business. The study conducted by the commission found that the nation's best agencies consistently display nine best practices:

1. Focus on customer service and satisfaction

2. Frequent customer contact

3. Valued staff

4. Participatory management

5. Vision

6. Win-win supplier relationships

7. Efficient processes

8. Total account development

9. Continuous improvement

The IIAA's Best Practices efforts are not only an example of what can be done by insurance organizations to increase customer satisfaction but also serve as a goal and a resource to the insurance business as a whole.

[DA04484]

EMPOWERMENT

Leaders often provide for the orderly dispersal of authority by empowering employees.

Empowerment

The distribution of authority, resources, information, and accountability to employees in an organization in order to make decisions and to solve problems.

Empowerment means releasing and channeling the potential but underused energy and skills of employees. For empowerment to be successful, three elements are required—alignment, capability, and trust. A compliance-commitment scale is helpful to assess employees' cooperation.

One of the weaknesses of the movement toward continuous improvement is the language used to discuss and describe it. The language tends to be inflated and self-flattering, and it relies heavily on the use of jargon— buzzwords and catchwords—that suggest mere fads in "management theory." Talk of missions and visions can sound as if corporate executives need to combine the traits of Michael Jordan with those of Mother Teresa. Despite the associations of some of the lingo of continuous improvement, it describes work, the organization and operation of businesses. Similarly, the term "empowerment" now frequently causes people to shrug and roll their eyes. Although the word has rapidly become a cliché, it nonetheless tries to point to something real. That reality can be valuable. See the exhibit "The Exodus."

The Exodus

An Example of Lack of Empowerment

The president and chief executive officer (CEO) of an insurance organization was struck by the daily stampede of customer service representatives (CSRs) from their workstations to their cars in the parking lot at precisely 4:30 every afternoon. It became part of his own daily ritual, when he was in the office, to position himself so that he could observe the energetic exodus of employees.

One day he took his post, 4:30 came and went, but nothing happened. There was no mad rush of smiling, chatting people, reaching for keys and migrating to their cars. He decided to investigate.

He learned that one of the CSRs had become interested in a relief effort on behalf of people who had been struck by tragedy on the other side of the world. The CSRs were staying late to meet on their own time to plan a food, clothing, and fund-raising drive.

A good deal of thought and effort went into this campaign. CSRs displayed skills— arranging for the donation of trucking services, recruiting volunteers to pack and load the collected materials, maintaining financial records—they had never been called on to use at work. The president had to admit to himself that he had assumed they lacked such skills and were not interested in developing them or using them. He had concluded all they wanted to do was put in their time at the office and rush out at quitting time. He realized his organization's CSRs represented an underused and misjudged potential reservoir of energy and skill. He started to think of ways to release and channel some of that energy on the job.

[DA04485]

Because empowerment means releasing and channeling the potential but underused energy and skills of employees, the key to empowerment, as this example suggests, is a change of heart or a change of mind on the part of someone in a position of authority. It is not a scheme for "fixing the worker bees" or trying to get more out of employees while looking at them in the way they have always been viewed or treating them in the way they have always been treated. Empowerment means sharing power by granting employees more authority and responsibility so that work becomes one dignified way for them to achieve their potential and lead meaningful lives. Work can be, like family life, community service, hobbies, recreational activities, and so on, one of the ways people develop and find meaning.

But empowerment cannot be achieved by simply "turning employees loose" or "getting out of the way" of employees. Such an approach represents an abdication of responsibility rather than an orderly dispersal of authority and is likely to merely cause confusion. Three elements—alignment, capability, and trust—are required for empowerment to succeed.

Alignment

One of the roles of leadership is to "align." A primary reason for developing mission statements; vision statements; and statements of values, goals, and objectives is to align employees—that is, to ensure that all employees understand not only their specific tasks and how they should be accomplished but also why they are performed. In this way, the specific tasks performed are seen as part of a larger whole—fulfilling the organization's purpose—in such a way that the organization will move toward its vision. Without **alignment**, empowered employees have no way of knowing what they should do, why they should do it, or whether they are doing it well. True alignment—a shared vision— encourages commitment rather than compliance from employees, a desire to contribute to the organization's mission rather than a grudging willingness to do what is demanded. A compliance-commitment scale, showing the range from compliance to commitment, is helpful to assess the cooperation of employees. See the exhibit "The Compliance-Commitment Scale Toward an Organization's Mission."

Alignment
Ensures that employees understand their tasks, how the tasks should be accomplished, and why the tasks are performed (what to do, how to do it, and why they are doing it).

Capability

Truly aligned and empowered employees can still be limited by their ability, skill, knowledge, and the design of the processes within which they operate as well as by the materials and equipment with which they do their jobs. Hiring practices, training, and the allocation of physical resources are all needed to ensure that empowered employees are capable of performing their jobs.

The Compliance-Commitment Scale Toward an Organization's Mission

Commitment	Desires outcome to occur. Will do whatever it takes.
Enrollment	Desires outcome to occur. Will do whatever needs to be done within reasonable means.
Genuine Compliance	Understands the benefits of the outcome. Does everything expected and goes the second mile.
Formal Compliance	Generally sees the benefits of the mission. Does what is required, but nothing extra.
Grudging Compliance	Does not understand the benefits of the mission. Begrudgingly does what is required.
Noncompliance	Does not understand the benefits of the mission. Resists aligning self with the mission.
Apathy	Completely indifferent. Neither for or against aligning self with the mission.

Adapted from Peter M. Senge, The Fifth Discipline (New York: Doubleday, 1990). [DA04486]

Trust

Many of the attitudes in the workplace are now anachronistic. They stem from a time when unskilled workers were constantly watched by supervisors—the word literally means "overseers"—to ensure that they were productive. That situation was based on and reinforced by mutual distrust. The result was often con jobs, conflicts, or both. Nonetheless, that system worked well for years, and America's industrial wealth was to a large extent produced by it. In addition, many of today's managers and executives emerged from and were successful in organizations that were shaped by that system and its assumptions.

Mutual distrust—con jobs and conflicts—now tends to produce merely wasted effort and unnecessarily unpleasant working conditions. Employees who know what their jobs are, know why they are important, know how to do them well, and are supplied with the training and resources to do them well will only be frustrated and hampered in their efforts if they are not trusted by supervisors, managers, and executives.

On the other hand, employees who cannot trust an organization's management will never be truly aligned with the organization's mission and vision. Mutual trust cannot be purchased or commanded. It must be earned. Its development can take a great deal of time and effort, but it should be the result of leadership. Empowered employees, like satisfied customers, are the proof of organizational leadership.

TEAMS

The formation of a team is often a way for an executive, a manager, or a supervisor to delegate authority.

Leaders often provide for the orderly dispersal of authority by empowering employees. Empowered employees frequently work most effectively in teams. Increased employee involvement often leads to an increased use of teams.

The use of teams in the workplace is an attempt to organize in a way that is conducive to continuous improvement because teams have the potential to be oriented toward customers, improve processes, and increase employee involvement. But too often teams are thought of in only one way, that is, as highly autonomous groups consisting of members who are more or less equals. There are actually many types of teams, reflecting the different types of work teams do.

A team can be defined as a group of individuals working toward a common goal. The goal of the team and the kind of work required to achieve it help to determine the nature and structure of the team.

Issuing insurance policies, deciding whether or not to write business in a specific geographic territory, settling a claim, developing a new product, designing a marketing campaign for a new product, and planning an organization's annual picnic are all different kinds of jobs that can be performed by different kinds of teams. The organization and nature of the team should depend on its goal. The duration of a team's existence, its level of autonomy, and the roles of the individual members cannot be predetermined in a vacuum. Nonetheless, there are guidelines that can be useful for all teams.

The formation of a team does not replace the responsibility of management but provides another way of fulfilling it. As a result, management remains responsible for clearly stating what is expected of the team and establishing limits within which the team can operate. Management must also supply the team with all of the information and resources it will need to perform its function and achieve its goal.

Team members themselves or the relevant manager often develop a written charter for a newly formed team. Team charters are used to state these attributes:

- The problem to be addressed
- The expected outcome
- The limits to the team's activities and authority

A **team charter** is a small-scale equivalent of an organization's mission, vision, values, goals, and objectives. The problem to be addressed defines the team's mission or purpose. The expected outcome provides the team with a concrete picture of the future, a vision. The limits set on the team's activities and authority are equivalent to its values, goals, and objectives. The amount of

Team charter

A team's mission, vision, values, goals, and objectives.

managerial involvement in the drafting of the charter varies greatly, depending on the culture of the organization.

Organizations generally use teams to increase customer satisfaction or improve processes while reducing costs. The benefits of a team for customers and the organization should be, and usually are, clear. But team members should also benefit from their participation, and those benefits should be spelled out. Benefits for team members can be monetary rewards, recognition, the development of new skills, an improved work life, the opportunity to engage in or get a feel for a new and different operating area of the organization, special privileges, tokens of appreciation, and feelings of contribution and accomplishment. Participation in a team should have clear benefits for all concerned, and those benefits should be communicated.

Few things can undermine the use of teams more than management's inability or unwillingness to acknowledge or act on recommendations or proposals emerging from a team. The decision to implement, modify, or reject a team's recommendation should come rapidly and with a full explanation to team members of the reasons for the decision. If the efforts of teams disappear into the limbo of subjects never again to be discussed, the organization probably is not yet ready for the use of teams and, in any case, is unlikely to be able to recruit willing participants in the future. Management must recognize and communicate the efforts of teams.

A team member's success should not be determined solely by the outcome of the team's work. Team members should be evaluated on (1) knowledge and support of the team's goals; (2) performance as a team member through proper allocation of time, serving as discussion leader for the team or taking minutes, coaching other team members, and contributing to the development of an appropriate process for the team's work; (3) skills and knowledge attained; (4) willingness to innovate and question traditional approaches taken by the organization; and (5) achievement of the goal of the team.

Team successes should be celebrated, often in a forum that provides public recognition for team members. The story of the team's success should be circulated throughout the organization or department. In this way, not only are team members rewarded, but also other employees learn from the experience.

Team Development

Some teams are "permanent," while others are organized to tackle a specific goal within a specified period of time. In either case, teams change over time. There are identifiable stages in team development. Being aware of these stages can increase the effectiveness of teams. B. W. Tuckerman, in "Development in Small Groups," defined four stages of team development:

1. Forming
2. Storming
3. Norming
4. Performing

Forming

At first, team members must form new relationships and mutually define their jobs and how to go about doing them. In many cases, individuals are unsure about why the team was formed and whether it can be successful. The support from management—the charter, the provision of necessary information and resources—is critical at this stage. The manager who called for the formation of the team is usually most heavily involved at the forming stage.

Storming

Conflicts are bound to arise among team members. Differing views of the team's goal, how to best achieve it, the assignment of tasks, and the assumption of roles and responsibilities necessarily lead to debates; argument; and, at times, hostility. Ground rules should be developed, perhaps with the assistance of the manager who formed the team, so that the storming stage remains constructive and discussion and debate center on issues rather than personalities. Brainstorming techniques, voting on decisions, and the reliance on data as the basis of decisions can help the team to emerge from the storming stage ready to work and progress. This is not to suggest that the storming stage of team development is irrelevant or does not represent "work." On the contrary, storming is a necessary part of the team's activities that can be frustrating for team members and managers alike simply because there are so few overt signs of progress during it. In many cases, the manager or team leader serves as a referee during the storming stage of team development.

Norming

The team becomes an integrated whole, working together, at this stage. Members share information and personal experiences, help each other, and take pride in working well together. The team progresses toward the goal, and the morale of the team improves. At this stage, managers who form teams and take an active part in them as facilitators or team leaders might become team members, simply remain available to the team as a resource as needed, or withdraw altogether.

Performing

At this stage, the team becomes self-directed and steadily progresses toward its goal. Team members now know their individual strengths and weaknesses and make the most of them by shifting roles and responsibilities naturally, almost as if doing so were second nature. The level of cooperation is high, and results include the discovery of innovative solutions to problems.

The manager who formed the team, if still involved, serves as a coach—giving advice and making suggestions—but is not active in the routine operations of the team.

As this description of the stages of team development clarifies, the role of the supervisor, manager, or executive who forms the team is crucial to the team's success but can vary widely. By establishing the team's charter, providing information and resources, and guiding the team, directly or indirectly, through the first two stages of team development, supervisory personnel at all levels can demonstrate leadership and contribute to the organization's efforts at continuous improvement by modeling the roles performed by senior management.

ORGANIZATIONAL STRUCTURES

Organizations that are dedicated to customer service are better positioned to meet their goals if they have involved, satisfied, and dedicated employees and the organizational structure to complement the employees' efforts to operate efficiently. Many organizations are using various organizational structures to balance leadership and employee involvement.

Organization structures within an organization are many and varied. These are some of the more common organizational structures:

- Pyramid structure
- **Inverted pyramid**
- **Concentric rings**
- **Networks, or matrix structures**

Inverted pyramid
An organizational structure that places customers at the top and works down to senior management.

Concentric rings
An organizational structure that places leadership at the center and works outward to customers.

Networks (matrix structures)
An organizational structure that involves small, autonomous units loosely joined.

Empowering employees and encouraging them to work in teams are two ways for organizations to achieve employee involvement. The present structures of many business organizations, however, often work against employee involvement and must change if continuous improvement efforts are to be successful.

The shift from management to leadership, with its resultant shift from low to high levels of employee involvement, implies a change in the structure of the organization. This shift is predicated on a customer orientation, on the realization that an organization's revenues are derived from satisfied customers, and on the realization that customers can best be satisfied by the collective result of the actions of individual employees.

Pyramid Structure

The emphasis on management with a low level of employee involvement found expression in hierarchical organizational structures. Organizational charts often took the form of pyramids. The CEO was at the top of the pyramid, supported by levels of managers and supervisors, all of which rested on a wide base of uninvolved employees. See the exhibit "Pyramid Structure."

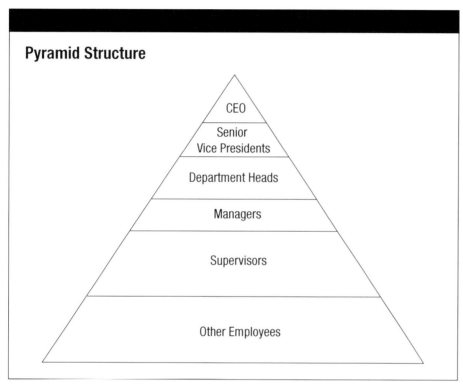

Pyramid Structure

[DA04488]

Such structures worked well for industrial organizations with an internal orientation that could succeed by defining quality as "conformance to specifications." Frequently, such organizations enjoyed a quasi or temporary monopoly and could afford to support a bureaucratic structure that operated in a stable marketplace. As customers found or demanded more and more choices and as the technological and economic environment became less stable, pyramid structures were stretched or shaken. The appropriate structures for organizations now reflect the need for flexibility, the ability to adapt to changes rapidly to identify and satisfy changing customer needs and expectations.

Inverted Pyramids

One element in the redesign of organizational structures is the wish to include customers in them, formally recognizing the importance of customers to the organization. This wish led some people to experiment with inverted pyramids. In an inverted pyramid, the customers are at the top of the organizational structure followed by the employees who have the most frequent and direct contact with customers—salespeople, marketing representatives, customer service representatives (CSRs), and so on. At the bottom is the senior management team that is responsible for deciding the overall strategy and policies of the organization, including which markets to serve and which products and services to offer. See the exhibit "Inverted Pyramid."

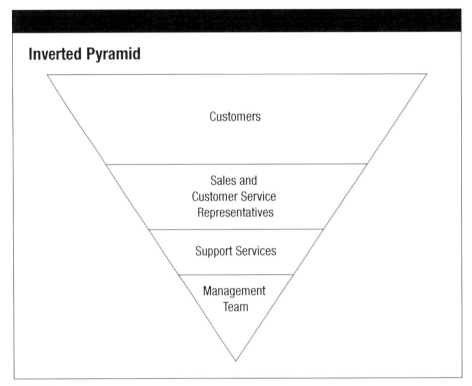

Inverted Pyramid

Customers

Sales and
Customer Service
Representatives

Support Services

Management
Team

[DA04492]

Concentric Rings

Some organizations found that concentric rings better reflect the connection among customers, front-line employees, internal services, and the organization's leadership. Concentric rings emphasize the relationship between internal and external customers and the need for satisfaction to move outward, from the leadership, through employees, to customers. See the exhibit "Concentric Rings."

Networks

Some organizations are finding that networks, which involve the division of the organization into small, autonomous units, loosely joined, provide the most effective structure. This is particularly true for organizations that serve

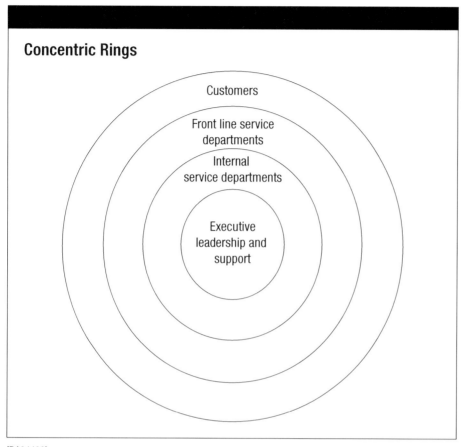

Concentric Rings

[DA04493]

very different groups of customers. A graphic representation of a network, or matrix can be shown in a graph. See the exhibit "Network."

No one organizational structure is right for all organizations. In fact, the depiction of the structures is less important than whether the structure reflects governing ideas of the organization as embodied in its mission, vision, values, goals, and objectives. Organizations with committed leaders who are capable of inspiring commitment from employees should have few problems finding a satisfactory organizational structure.

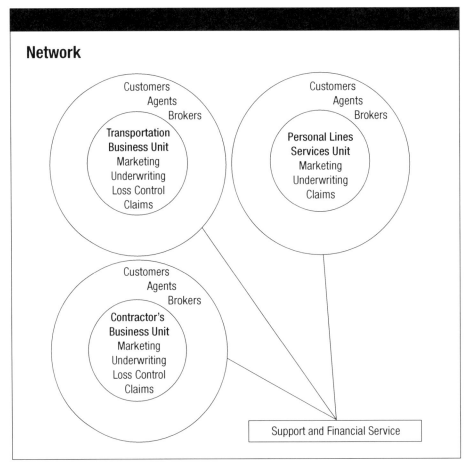

Network

Customers
Agents
Brokers
Transportation Business Unit
Marketing
Underwriting
Loss Control
Claims

Customers
Agents
Brokers
Personal Lines Services Unit
Marketing
Underwriting
Claims

Customers
Agents
Brokers
Contractor's Business Unit
Marketing
Underwriting
Loss Control
Claims

Support and Financial Service

[DA04495]

SUMMARY

One of the tenets of continuous improvement is that customers can best and most consistently be satisfied only by involved, satisfied employees. Developing a staff of involved employees requires leadership. Leadership differs from management in that the aim of leadership is the improvement of systems while the aim of management is to achieve results. Both functions are necessary, but continuous improvement requires an increased emphasis on leadership. The functions of management are to plan, organize, direct, coordinate, and control. The roles of leadership are to envision, align, empower, coach, and care.

The shift toward leadership shows itself in several ways. First, organizations now often draft mission statements; vision statements; and statements of values, goals, and objectives as a way to increase employee involvement.

Employees who are aligned, capable, and trusted are empowered. A compliance-commitment scale is useful to assess the cooperation of employees.

Empowered employees frequently work most effectively in teams. Increased employee involvement often leads to an increased use of teams. The four stages of team development are forming, storming, norming, and performing.

Employee involvement often brings about changes in organizational structures. The hierarchical, bureaucratic structures of the past—the pyramids of the traditional organizational chart—work against employee involvement. Many organizations are now experimenting with a variety of alternatives to such traditional structures, such as inverted pyramids, concentric rings, and matrix structures.

The ideas that provide the foundation for employee involvement, the empowerment of employees, the use of teams, and changes in organizational structures, all follow directly from the need to identify and satisfy the rapidly changing needs of customers.

ASSIGNMENT NOTES

1. Lynne Goch, "Surpassing Lane," Best's Review, October 1999, p. 62.
2. Peter Senge, The Fifth Discipline (New York: Doubleday, 1990), pp. 217-218.

Checking on Progress

Educational Objectives

After learning the content of this assignment, you should be able to:

▷ Describe the five stages of maturation.

▷ Describe the role of awards in the evaluation of continuous improvement efforts.

Checking on Progress

9

MATURATION

Organizations engaging in continuous improvement move through five stages of maturity. There is no time limit set for each of these stages or even a suggestion of how long it typically takes organizations to move from one stage to the next. The emphasis is on the characteristics of each stage and the apparent need for all organizations that pursue continuous improvement to move through all of the stages.

Researchers have found that organizations mature with respect to continuous improvement by moving through five distinct stages:

1. Consensus
2. Education
3. Problem solving
4. Deployment
5. Integration

Each stage has identifiable characteristics.

Consensus

The first stage in continuous improvement is marked by the achievement of a consensus by the organization's top management. Such a consensus means that all of the organization's top managers are united in their commitment to transforming the organization by adopting a customer orientation, improving processes, and increasing employee involvement.

Because consensus represents only an intention to begin the continuous improvement journey, management tends to take it for granted. Actually, building a consensus that represents a commitment is difficult to do and takes time and energy. However, little, if anything, can be done without it. In addition, an apparent consensus can easily break down once the members of the top management team understand precisely what the commitment to continuous improvement involves.

Although the response to the ideas of continuous improvement is often positive and enthusiastic, the number of organizations that have successfully implemented the principles of continuous improvement remains relatively low, particularly in the insurance business. Sometimes, consensus on the commitment to continuous improvement comes only with the realization by members of the top management team that trying to maintain any other kind of organization either cannot be done or is not worth doing.

Education

The second stage of organizational maturation is characterized by the education of all employees of an organization in the principles of continuous improvement—the emphasis on customers, the techniques for process improvement, and the rationale for employee involvement—as well as data-gathering methods and statistical tools. Organizations that are committed to continuous improvement are sometimes described as **learning organizations**. One reason for this is that continuous improvement necessitates and relies on organization-wide education. In addition, the organization's mission, vision, and values, along with departmental and individual goals and objectives, must be learned.

Learning organizations
Those organizations in which people, individually and collectively, continually improve their capacity to produce results and to expand their patterns of thinking.

The educational effort required by organizations can help to energize them and make them vibrant. The atmosphere associated with continuous improvement is often described as innovative. Innovation often comes about as an immediate response to the ability to see the obvious clearly.

Consensus by top management to a commitment to continuous improvement should precede organization-wide education because that educational effort takes time, has costs, and leads to a change in the culture of an organization that the leadership should not only expect but also desire.

Problem Solving

The third stage of organizational maturation begins when employees start to apply what they have learned. Frequently at this stage, the techniques of continuous improvement are applied within departments or functional areas. To do this, teams of employees, sometimes called quality circles, attempt to improve a specific process or increase customer satisfaction in a specific way.

One of the difficulties faced by the organization's leadership at this stage is the need to set priorities. Initial improvement efforts must be successful. The organization must be able to engage in improvement efforts while continuing to meet the needs of customers. Sometimes the future organization must take shape while the current organization continues to perform. Selecting specific improvement efforts that will build the confidence of employees and move the organization toward its future method of operations, yet not cause confusion or jeopardize current levels of service, is one of the most difficult decisions the organization's leadership must make.

The problem-solving stage of maturation nears its end when numerous, if not all, departments and functional areas have made clear improvements. What is more, these improvements are incorporated into the day-to-day operations while the remnants of earlier methods of operation—parallel systems that were temporarily maintained, for instance—begin to disappear.

Deployment

The fourth stage of organizational maturity, deployment, represents a culmination of the first three stages and is often seen as a "breakthrough" stage. It is characterized by the implementation and coordination of continuous improvement techniques throughout the entire organization. As a result, it is represented by tackling cross-functional and inter-departmental problems. Changes in organizational structure frequently become necessary during the deployment stage of organizational maturation. In many ways, this stage most severely tests the commitment of the organization's leadership.

What should strengthen the resolve of an organization's leadership and employees alike is the realization that any organization that has reached the deployment stage of maturation is well on its way to delivering high-quality service.

Integration

The fifth stage of organizational maturation, integration, is characterized by the complete merger of the organization's business strategy with its continuous improvement efforts. This merger is epitomized by the disappearance of any separate structures—quality circles, an executive or a department dedicated to continuous improvement, parallel systems, and so on. Instead, policies, structures, and systems are integrated to do business through the use of continuing improvement efforts.

Very few organizations reach the integration stage. The reason should be clear—the changing environments in which permanent organizations operate make the complete integration of continuous improvement and the business strategy extremely difficult.

A weakness in this description of the stages of organization maturation is that it describes the movement retrospectively, making an orderly, linear process out of what once seemed chaotic and frustrating. Despite that weakness, it does provide organizations with a way of checking on their progress.[1] See the exhibit "Common Obstacles to Maturation."

Common Obstacles to Maturation

Obstacles to continuous improvement maturation turn up in all types of organizations and under all kinds of conditions. These common obstacles can be readily identified and therefore avoided. Although they are most often discussed in terms of process improvement alone, they are relevant to all continuous improvement efforts. Furthermore, these obstacles most often emerge when organizations attempt to skip or ignore one of the stages of organizational maturity. The obstacles, known by various names and descriptions, are:

- Tampering
- Incomplete ownership
- Lack of expertise
- Imposed solutions
- Artificial constraints
- World hunger

Tampering occurs when top management targets a specific incident or problem for improvement while ignoring the fact that the underlying process is incapable of producing the desired results. Tampering can cause frustration for participants and mask the real problem and, thus, postpone if not prevent its solution.

Incomplete ownership arises from a failure to identify and consider all stakeholders. The consensus achieved by top management can soon be fragmented if the financial stakeholders in an organization, for example, are antagonistic to the commitment to continuous improvement.

Lack of expertise is an obstacle when the second stage of maturity, education, is minimized or bypassed. In any case, situations often arise that require special expertise, and many organizations avoid this obstacle by prudently seeking the advice or services of outside consultants or investing in special training for selected employees.

An imposed solution usually results from a lack of commitment on the part of the organization's leadership. The lack of commitment shows itself by the leadership using continuous improvement efforts as a disguise when implementing a predetermined plan of action chosen by the leadership without an understanding of the underlying processes and problems.

Artificial constraints come about when expectations for continuous improvement activities are unrealistic and established without a full understanding of the root causes of organizational problems. Artificial constraints can arise from the attempt to bypass or abbreviate the third stage of maturity, problem solving. The knowledge and experience gained by process improvement successes within departments or functional areas are usually necessary before realistic expectations for cross-functional efforts can be established.

World hunger means that the aim is so broad and general, the problem to be tackled is so deeply ingrained in an organization, and authority or ownership is so diffused or confused that continuous improvement efforts tend to be stymied. Under these circumstances, if the organization's leadership achieves consensus, it is a pseudo consensus.

Although all continuous improvement efforts include setbacks and frustrations, an awareness of these common obstacles to success can assist in their identification and avoidance.

[DA04496]

AWARDS

Competing for quality awards is a distinctive way that organizations can track the progress of continuous improvement. Awards can also provide an increased understanding of the concepts and techniques used in continuous improvement efforts and further inspire organizations to engage in these efforts.

Organizations can compete for awards based on continuous improvement criteria. These awards have often been offered to encourage organizations to learn about and pursue continuous improvement. Perhaps the most prestigious award of this type in the United States is the Malcolm Baldrige National Quality Award. A similar award, specifically intended for organizations that provide insurance and risk management services, is the Arthur Quern Quality Award.

A way for organizations to check on progress is for them to compete for one or more of the awards that have been established to recognize achievement in continuous improvement. Competing for such awards has advantages.

First, competing requires an analysis of the organization's efforts by outside observers who are familiar with similar efforts by other organizations in a wide variety of fields. In effect, competition for the award becomes a kind of benchmarking. Second, preparation for the competition can reinforce the commitment of the organization's leadership to continuous improvement efforts and serve as a signal to employees that the leadership is proud of what has been accomplished. Finally, the possibility of external recognition of the organization's achievements can boost employee morale.

Probably the best known and most prestigious of these awards in the U.S. is the **Malcolm Baldrige National Quality Award**. Motorola's reputation for its continuous improvement efforts grew in part because it was an early winner of the Baldrige Award. United Services Automobile Association (USAA), a leader in continuous improvement efforts among insurance organizations, has competed for the Baldrige Award and has been recognized with a site visit—clearly setting it apart from a vast number of organizations that compete for the award.

Many such awards are now offered from a variety of sources and for a number of purposes. One such award has been established specifically for the risk management and insurance field. The Risk and Insurance Management Society (RIMS) and the Quality Insurance Congress (QIC) cosponsor the annual **Arthur Quern Quality Award**, named in memory of the former chairman and chief executive of Aon Risk Services. The purpose of the award is to "highlight individuals, products or companies with a demonstrated commitment to quality." ECS, Inc., which specializes in the integrated management of environmental risk, was nominated for the award by a client and was among the first winners of the award.

Malcolm Baldrige National Quality Award

An award designed to increase awareness of continuous improvement techniques among businesses in the United States.

Arthur Quern Quality Award

An award designed to increase awareness of continuous improvement among organizations involved in risk management and insurance.

SUMMARY

Organizations that undertake continuous improvement initiatives generally move through five stages of maturation. How these stages proceed in an organization and the duration of each stage vary depending on the organization's specific characteristics.

Competing for awards entails an evaluation of an organization's continuous improvement efforts by an outside, objective source. The criteria for such awards provide performance measures worthy of consideration by organizations that pursue continuous improvement.

ASSIGNMENT NOTE

1.   This discussion is based on Arthur R. Tenner and Irving J. DeToro, Total Quality Management, IIA Edition (Reading, Mass.: Addison-Wesley, 1994), pp. 184-185.

Index

Page numbers in boldface refer to pages where the word or phrase is defined.